EDITOR: Maryanne Blacker

DESIGN DIRECTOR: Neil Carlyle

■ ■ ■

ASSISTANT EDITOR: Judy Newman

SUB-EDITOR: Danielle Farah

ART DIRECTOR: Robbylee Phelan

CADET ARTIST: Louise McGeachie

SECRETARY: Wendy Moore

■ ■ ■

DESIGNER: Paula Rizzuto

■ ■ ■

CONTRIBUTORS: Lynn Humphries, Diane Wallis
Louise Patniotis, Alan Hill

ILLUSTRATORS: Diane Bradley,
Louise Tuckwell: illustrations in "Food Facts"

PHOTOGRAPHER: Rodney Weidland

COVER PHOTOGRAPHER: Per Ericson

■ ■ ■

PUBLISHER: Richard Walsh

DEPUTY PUBLISHER: Graham Lawrence

EDITOR-IN-CHIEF: Sandra Funnell

■ ■ ■

Produced by The Australian Women's Weekly
Home Library
Typeset by Letter Perfect, Sydney.
Printed by Dai Nippon Co Ltd, Tokyo, Japan
Published by Australian Consolidated Press,
54 Park Street Sydney
Distributed by Network Distribution Company,
54 Park Street Sydney
Distributed in the U.K. by Australian Consolidated Press (UK)
Ltd (0604) 760 456. Distributed in New Zealand by Gordon
and Gotch (NZ) Ltd (09) 654 379. Distributed in Canada
by Whitecap Books Ltd (604) 980 9852. Distributed in South
Africa by Intermag (011) 493 3200.

■ ■ ■

© A C P 1990

Household Manual.

Includes index.
ISBN 0949892 79 3.

1. Home economics - Handbooks,
manuals, etc. (Series: Australian
Women's Weekly Home Library).
640.

■ ■ ■

THE HOUSEHOLD MANUAL

Crammed with useful tips and techniques the Household Manual is an important addition to your home. We've included practical hints on storing food, making the most of your microwave and freezer and choosing wine to have with meals; there's information on the basic cuts of meat and how to cook them, preparing fish and shelling prawns. The budding home handyperson can learn how to change tap washers and repair fuses and do those simple but annoying electrical and plumbing jobs. We tell you how to remove all manner of stains, look after those treasured keepsakes and deal with household pests. Instant advice is now on hand!

KITCHEN SENSE

The kitchen can be a source of inspiration for some and fill others with a sense of fear and loathing. A little organisation can go a long way to helping you enjoy the time you spend in the kitchen, or at least make you more comfortable in it.

Maintaining a healthy stock of standbys in the pantry, freezer and refrigerator is easy if you know how! And, surround yourself with good kitchen equipment – we tell you how to choose the right saucepans and knives and how to look after them properly – it will make things easier.

In this chapter we reveal the mysteries of **all** those cooking oils and their uses, and just what those "strange" ingredients from other countries look like and why they are added to certain dishes.

There are fundamentals too – cup and spoon measurements, oven temperatures and a conversion table from old measures to metric. We tell you how to make the most of your freezer and microwave and remind you about the need for hygiene in your kitchen at all times.

Remember, everyday items can be dangerous, be careful not to have pan handles overhanging the edge of the stove, do not leave hot oil unattended or knives lying around on benchtops within reach of curious little fingers.

THE BEST OIL FOR THE JOB

Oils differ in their flavours, appearance, cooking applications and storage requirements. There are three basic types: polyunsaturated, mono-unsaturated and saturated.

☞ Scientific research has established that polyunsaturated oils such as sunflower, safflower, maize (corn), grapeseed and soy bean are more helpful in controlling blood cholesterol and triglyceride levels (the risk factors in cardiovascular diseases) than saturated fats such as coconut and palm oil. Mono-unsaturated oils such as peanut and olive oil are considered to have an intermediate effect.

☞ The National Heart Foundation of Australia recommends that oils be used in moderation: one to two tablespoons per day of the poly-unsaturated varieties - less if you are overweight. The Association produces numerous publications giving dietary advice and has offices in each State.

☞ Restrict your use of deep-frying and shallow-frying as cooking methods. They can easily increase the fat content of your diet above the recommended 30 per cent of total kilojoules. Stir-frying uses relatively little oil.

☞ It is important to use the oil best suited to each recipe. For example, if you are greasing a mould or baking tin for a fruit mousse or cakes, use a light, polyunsaturated oil such as safflower. Olive oil, or any of the nut oils, are too strongly flavoured and will affect the taste of the finished dish.

BLENDED VEGETABLE OILS: a mixture of two or more oils, they can be polyunsaturated or saturated. They are inexpensive and not usually highly refined – refining adds to the cost. Use for frying or roasting. Avoid mixing them with other ingredients, as in cakes and dressings, as they can develop an unpleasant taste.

COCONUT: a saturated oil used in S.E. Asian, Indian and Pacific cooking. Some people find it hard to digest. If a recipe calls for a coconut flavour, try using coconut milk or cream instead. Coconut oil is used in vegetable cooking fats and in margarines.

CORN: see Maize.

GRAPESEED: a pleasant, light, very pale green oil that is ideal for salad dressings, roasting vegetables and deep-frying (it has a high smoking point of 230 degrees Celsius).

MAIZE: also known as corn oil. A by-product of the manufacture of cornflour, this polyunsaturated oil is good for frying.

NUT (Almond, Hazel and Walnut): these are among the most unstable of oils as they go rancid quickly and spoil if overheated. Buy them in small quantities and store in a cool place. They are also expensive. Hazel and walnut oils are popular in French cooking and are a delicious addition to salad dress-

ings. The flavour can be quite pronounced, but the intensity does vary, depending on where it was produced.

OLIVE: a mono-unsaturated, nutritious oil which no good cook should be without. It can be used in all forms of cooking, although it should be avoided for deep-frying as it has a low flashpoint. Spanish, Greek, French and Italian olive oils come in a tremendous range of aromas, flavours and consistencies. Acidity is the standard by which olive oils are judged – the greater the acid content, the lower the standard. There are virgin olive oils (taken from the first pressing of the olives) and refined olive oils (taken from the residual pulp of the first pressing). The virgin olive oils can be as expensive as good wine. Colours vary from greenish gold to pale yellow.

PALM: a saturated oil from the fruit of the African oil palm. There is also a more delicately flavoured palm kernel oil which is expressed from the kernels only. Palm oils have a distinctive aroma. They are commonly used in margarines and shortenings. Used for frying.

PEANUT (Groundnut): a light, mono-unsaturated oil, often used in stir-fry recipes. Will last for three-to-five fryings. Also good for salad dressings.

SAFFLOWER: the highest in polyunsaturates and the lowest in saturates of all the commercial vegetable oils. Suitable for salad dressings, cakes and marinades. High in Vitamin E.

SESAME: a golden-brown oil with a delicate nutty flavour. Use a few drops to flavour another oil when cooking, otherwise the taste will be too strong. Used for frying and salad dressings.

SOLID VEGETABLE OILS: these oils have been processed to make them solid at room temperature. Wrap carefully and store in the refrigerator; they will keep for several months without going rancid. Used for deep-frying. High in saturated fat.

SOY BEAN: high in polyunsaturates. Has a short shelf-life. Often used for blending with other oils. Although nutritionally excellent, in its pure form it has a slightly unpleasant smell. Used for deep- and shallow-frying.

SUNFLOWER: an oil that is high in polyunsaturates, it is also highly nutritious. Used in dressings.

KITCHEN EQUIPMENT

Always buy the best equipment, cheap goods rarely last long.

SAUCEPANS AND KNIVES

Good-quality equipment can't make you a better cook, but it will make tasks easier. Think of kitchen utensils as an investment. Maintain them carefully and they will reward you with many years of service.

SAUCEPANS

Metals, durability, ease of maintenance, cost, weight, non-stick coatings and visual appearance are all factors that influence your decision when buying saucepans.

ALUMINIUM: a very good conductor of heat. Strong, lightweight, non-rusting. This metal will darken some foods such as spinach. Avoid leaving food standing in aluminium pans too long as the metal can impart a very slight metallic taste.
To clean: wash in hot, soapy water. You can use the dishwasher, but any anodised surface colouring will eventually wear away. To remove any tarnish, fill the pan with water, add a little vinegar and boil for 15 minutes.

COPPER: one of the best conductors of heat. Available lined with stainless steel (which is very hard-wearing) or with tin (which needs replacing periodically). Unlined copper gives food an unpleasant taste. The only copper utensil left unlined is the bowl for whisking egg whites – the metal reacts chemically with the whites, resulting in a greater volume than is otherwise possible. Copper pans are expensive and need regular polishing.
To clean: take equal parts salt, flour and vinegar, plus one egg white. Mix to a paste. Rub on to the copper with kitchen paper, leave a few minutes, wash off in hot soapy water, rinse, dry. Polish with a soft cloth. Do not put copper in the dishwasher.

IRON: a good conductor of heat, iron is strong but heavy. It must be seasoned to prevent rust (see how to clean section, below). Enamelled cast-iron saucepans look very attractive; take care not to chip them. Unprotected cast iron will discolour dishes containing wine, tomatoes and vinegar, while these three ingredients tend to remove the seasoning, making food stick to the pan. Iron is good for frying pans as it retains heat well. Black iron or carbon-steel frying pans are lighter than cast iron, but also need regular seasoning.
To clean: season the pan when new. Dip a piece of kitchen paper in oil and wipe it over the interior. Pour in a little more oil to cover the bottom of the pan; place over a medium heat until the oil begins to smoke. Remove from heat, cool, wipe out any remaining oil. Put in a layer of salt, heat again until salt starts to turn brown. Cool, rinse out salt, dry. Repeat the oiling and heating process (not the salt process). Your pan is now seasoned and ready for use. Also use this seasoning method for woks.

After use, simply wipe out the pan with kitchen paper dipped in oil. Food particles can be soaked off by adding a little water to the pan and simmering for a few minutes. Rinse, dry, rub over with a little oil.

NON-STICK SURFACES: very useful for those trying to cut down on fat in cooking. Don't place over high heat for prolonged periods as this will shorten the life of the coating. Use plastic or wooden implements to avoid scratches. Non-stick coatings don't discolour or taint food.
To clean: condition a new pan by applying a thin layer of oil with a paper towel. After use, wash in hot soapy water. Can be placed in the dishwasher. Wipe over the surface again with a thin layer of oil before putting the pan away. Remove stains with a nylon scourer.

STAINLESS STEEL: lightweight, strong, easy to clean, hard-wearing. As it is a poor conductor of heat on its own, it usually has a heat-conductive panel made of copper or aluminium applied to the base to make it very efficient.
To clean: can be put in a dishwasher. Very easy to clean in hot soapy water. Burnt-on food can be soaked and scrubbed off with a nylon scourer.

GLASS: A good conductor of heat, although not as efficient as metal. Use it for those items that need to be cooked in water or oils because the liquid itself distributes the heat effectively. Glass is ideal for anxious cooks who like to be able to see at a glance how a dish is progressing. To make viewing easy, some manufacturers of stainless-steel pans have produced ranges with lids made of toughened glass. Glass can go on the stove, in the oven and in the microwave. It is sufficiently good-looking to be used at the dining table as a serving dish. Because of their high acid content, uncooked marinades for meat, fish, vegetables and fruit should always be made in a glass, porcelain or glazed earthenware dish.
To clean: wash in hot soapy water after soaking off burnt-on food. Can be put in the dishwasher. Don't use harsh abrasives.

KNIVES

The best knives for the home cook are made of high carbon stainless steel. This is an alloy that combines the sharpness of carbon steel with the rust and stainproof qualities of stainless steel. Most modern knives labelled stainless steel are, in fact, made of high carbon stainless steel. Some brands are superior to others. If you are confued go to a specialist kitchen shop and ask for advice.
✏ Good-quality knives have a full "tang". This means the metal extension of the blade runs the full length of the handle and is visible around the sides of the handle. The tang should be fastened to the handle by rivets, not glue.
✏ Choose knives that are the correct

THE ESSENTIALS

- Baking or roasting tray
- Bottle opener
- Can opener
- Corkscrew
- Chopping board
- Cake tins
- Casserole dish with lid
- Citrus squeezer
- Egg slice
- Frying pan with lid
- Garlic crusher
- Grater
- Kettle
- Kitchen scissors
- Knives *(carving, vegetable and serrated see Knives left)*
- Ladle
- Measuring cups and spoons
- Measuring jug
- Mixing bowl
- Pastry brush
- Pie or flan dish
- Perforated or slotted spoon
- Potato masher
- Rolling pin
- Saucepans, two with lids *(see left)*
- Skewers
- Sieve
- Toaster
- Vegetable peeler
- Vegetable steamer
- Whisks *(wire and hand held)*
- Wooden spoons

OPTIONAL EXTRAS

- Blender
- Cake moulds
- Cake cooling rack
- Coffee percolator
- Colander
- Electric beater
- Food processor
- Microwave oven
- Omelette pan
- Pastry cutters
- Pressure cooker
- Saucepans, casseroles and oven dishes
- Scales
- Vegetable scrubbing brush
- Wok

CUP AND SPOON MEASUREMENTS

To ensure accuracy in your recipes use the standard metric measuring equipment approved by Standards Australia:

(a) 250 millilitre cup for measuring liquids. A litre jug (*capacity 4 cups*) is also available.

(b) a graduated set of four cups – measuring 1 cup, half, third and quarter cup – for items such as flour, sugar, etc. When measuring in these fractional cups level off at the brim.

(c) a graduated set of four spoons: tablespoon *(20 millilitre liquid capacity)*, teaspoon *(5 millilitre)*, half and quarter teaspoons. The Australian, British and American teaspoon each has 5ml capacity.

Approximate cup and spoon conversion chart

Australian	American & British
1 cup	1¼ cups
¾ cup	1 cup
⅔ cup	¾ cup
½ cup	⅔ cup
⅓ cup	½ cup
¼ cup	⅓ cup
2 tablespoons	¼ cup
1 tablespoon	3 teaspoons

ALL SPOON MEASUREMENTS ARE LEVEL.

Oven Temperatures

ELECTRIC	C°	F°
Very slow	120	250
Slow	150	300
Moderately slow	160-180	325-350
Moderate	180-200	375-400
Moderately hot	210-230	425-450
Hot	240-250	475-500
Very hot	260	525-550

GAS		
Very slow	120	250
Slow	150	300
Moderately slow	160	325
Moderate	180	350
Moderately hot	190	375
Hot	200	400
Very hot	230	450

weight for you to handle easily. Make sure your fingers fit comfortably around the handle. Take time to select the right knife – this is an investment, not an impulse buy.

✏ You don't need many knives. Start with a chef's knife that has a wide, triangular blade, 20 to 25 centimetres in length. Use it for chopping. Also buy a sharp-tipped paring knife with a 10cm blade. Use it for peeling, scraping, chopping and paring. As funds permit, invest in a utility knife with a 15 to 18 centimetre-long blade, and a carving knife with a 20 to 25 centimetre blade that is narrower than a chef's knife.

✏ Wipe knives with a damp cloth after use. Don't put in the dishwasher or subject them to extreme heat. Scour the metal with abrasives when necessary. Dry knives thoroughly and give them a few wipes with a steel before storing them well out of the reach of children.

✏ It's pointless buying good knives if you don't keep them sharp. Buy a good-quality steel with a handle guard for protecting your fingers. Ask your butcher to show you the correct way to use it. Sharpen knives frequently. A very dull edge is best sharpened on an abrasive stone, or taken to a professional knife sharpener.

MEASUREMENTS

When cooking, use the one system of measurement thoroughout; never mix the measurements. Many a culinary masterpiece has been ruined by chopping and changing from ounces to teaspoons to grams and back to the original measure. Invest in a set of measuring spoons and cups to ensure your recipes turn out exactly as they should.

COOKING AND SERVING

It's not a pleasant thought, but our hands are generally very dirty. Wash your hands before preparing food and after going to the toilet, emptying the garbage bin, blowing your nose or touching your hair or face during food preparation. Also, wash your hands after touching raw meat and raw vegetables. Use hot soapy water, then wipe your hands on disposable paper kitchen towels – tea-towels, aprons, cleaning cloths and sponges are havens for bacteria and should be avoided as much as possible.

✏ Keep the preparation of cooked food and raw food entirely separate to avoid cross-contamination. Use two chopping boards – one for raw food, one for cooked. Plastic chopping boards are easier to keep clean than wooden ones.

✏ Throw out washing-up water once it looks murky and turns cool. Very hot water kills bacteria, while warm water encourages their growth.

✏ Wash down kitchen surfaces regularly with very hot water and disinfectant that has been diluted to a solution recommended by the manufacturer. Refrigerators and freezers must be defrosted regularly and cleaned with bicarbonate of soda – don't use disinfectant as it can taint foodstuffs. Dry appliances thoroughly before returning food to them as bacteria love moist places.

✏ If you are reheating food, do so thoroughly to kill bacteria. Once reheated, don't store and reheat again.

✏ Defrost food completely before reheating if not, heat is wasted in melting ice rather than heating the food adequately and safely.

✏ Throw away thawed liquids from meat and poultry, and make sure they don't drip on other foods.

IMPERIAL TO METRIC

If you are using recipes written in Imperial measures, it is easy to convert to metric or vice versa. Here's a list of some handy conversions using measuring jugs or cups and spoons. It will make some sense of those "old" recipes.

IMPERIAL	METRIC
1 cup (8 fluid ounces)	¾ cup
¾ cup	⅔ cup
⅔ cup	½ cup
½ cup	⅓ cup
⅓ cup	¼ cup
¼ cup	2 tablespoons
½ pint (10 fluid ounces)	1 cup (250 ml)
¼ pint (5 fluid ounces)	½ cup (125 ml)
1 gill (¼ pint or 5 fluid ounces)	½ cup

ALWAYS CHECK THE FRONT OR BACK OF RECIPE BOOKS TO ESTABLISH WHETHER SPOON MEASURES ARE LEVEL OR ROUNDED.

BARBECUES: NEVER use flammable liquids to start your fire. Watch for sparks, particularly in dry or windy conditions. Keep a fire blanket or fire extinguisher nearby. Keep children away from the fire, and from matches.

CLEANING PRODUCTS: l o c k these away in cupboards children can't reach. Many of these products are poisonous. Never mix cleaning chemicals – some combinations produce poisonous fumes.

COOKING OIL: has the potential to cause disaster and is one of the most common causes of household fires.

- NEVER leave any oil unattended over heat. Each type of oil reaches flashpoint at a different temperature. Olive oil, for example, will catch fire at a much lower temperature than grapeseed or coconut oil. Over-heated oil begins smoking prior to reaching flashpoint. Remove the pan from the heat immediately.
- Restrict the number of times you re-use oil for frying. The temperature at which it will catch fire decreases with each successive frying. Solid oil and peanut oil lasts for three-to-five fryings, while polyunsaturated oils such as maize (corn) should only be used once or twice.
- Strain cooled oil that is to be re-used, to remove food particles. Any food particles remaining will go rancid, burn easily and set the pan alight. Store the oil, tightly covered, in the refrigerator.
- Never try to extinguish an oil fire with water. The oil will spit and boil over, and may cause severe burns and scalds.
- To put out an oil fire, reduce its oxygen supply by putting a lid on the pan, or smothering the flames with a thick, dry, woollen blanket. Never use cotton tea-towels – they are too thin and will catch fire. Never use damp cloths - they will cause a great upsurge of scalding steam. Fire blankets and fire extinguishers for domestic use are available. Consider buying one for your home.
- Keep a flour shaker beside the stove. Flour shaken over a flaming pan will suppress the flames to a certain extent, but using too much will make the oil splash.

KNIVES: keep sharp knives on a magnetic knife rack mounted on a wall, or in a slotted wooden block on a bench top. Make sure they are not accessible to small children.

PAN HANDLES: never leave a pan with its handle jutting out over the stove or work surface. A child can easily reach

STORAGE

- Store dry goods such as flour in airtight containers in the larder; never put new flour on top of old. Keep cupboards dry and clean. Clean them out at least once a month; removing crumbs and wiping sticky jars with a clean, damp cloth. It will help to keep pest infestations at bay if you have food well sealed and stored properly and cupboards are kept clean.
- Keep wholemeal flour and wheatgerm in the refrigerator during hot weather.
- Pantry shelves should be kept as cool as possible. If you don't have a pantry, keep packaged and dried food in a cool cupboard and perishables in the refrigerator.
- ALWAYS check the "use by" date and do not use outdated goods, you could end up with food poisoning.
- If well sealed, dried and packaged food will keep for up to 3 months.
- Coffee beans can be kept in airtight jars for up to 3 months.
- Store dried fruit, flour, pulses, rices and spices in cool, dry conditions. They will keep longer in dark jars.
- Ground spices do not keep well; use as soon as possible after buying.

- Spices will keep longer if bought whole.
- Once a can is opened, keep the remainder in a bowl in the refrigerator and eat within a day or so.
- Cakes and biscuits will keep for up to 4 weeks in airtight tins or jars. Always keep them separate. Fruit cakes keep for up to 6 months.
- Insects bring germs. So do household pets. Put fly-screens on the windows. Keep cats, dogs and birds out of the kitchen.
- Keep refrigerators at about 4 degrees Celsius, freezers at -18 degrees Celsius. Invest in a fridge or freezer thermometer if you're not sure what the numbering system on your appliance means. Many people turn the dial the wrong way and increase, rather than decrease, the temperature. Make sure your appliances are sited correctly and working efficiently. (See Conserving Energy in Repairs & Maintenance.)
- It is difficult to give hard and fast rules about how long various foods will keep in the refrigerator or freezer. Read the labelling, check the "use by" date, use your nose and eyes to check if all is well. Discard anything you feel uneasy about. It is always better to be safe than sorry. Write the date of preparation on properly wrapped, home-cooked

items stored in the freezer – as weeks pass, you will have no recollection of when you cooked them. (Details on storage of meat, cereals, fish and shellfish, cheese, milk, butter and fruit and vegetables are in the Food Facts chapter beginning on page 28.)

Load and unload your refrigerator in one go. Don't keep flapping the door open, causing the temperature to rise. Maintaining a steady, low temperature in the refrigerator is very important in controlling bacterial growth.

Air must be able to circulate between and around the items in your refrigerator. Don't jam them all in, one on top of the other.

Always store raw foods well away from cooked ones. Keep raw items at the bottom of the fridge to prevent them dripping on and contaminating other foods.

Some bottled foods don't contain preservatives and must be refrigerated. Check the label. Tinned foods will keep for a long time because they are sterilised during the manufacturing process. However, once open and exposed to air, the contents will quickly deteriorate.

If you're having a party and need to store a large amount of food in the fridge, turn the temperature down an hour or two before you put the extra food in. Hot food must not be put straight into the fridge, but must be cooled rapidly first to prevent bacterial growth. Immerse the base of the pan in ice water, replenishing frequently. Cook small batches of a recipe rather than one large dish that will take a long time to cool. The longer the cooling time, the more likely the growth of harmful bacteria.

Keep strong-smelling items well away from eggs and milk, to avoid tainting. Most foods should be covered with cling film or aluminium foil.

KITCHEN PANTRY

People who live well out of reach of a corner shop understand the importance of having a well-stocked kitchen cupboard, refrigerator and freezer. The following list of items may appear extensive, but it represents a valuable time-saving and cost-saving asset. You'll have the basis for many meals at your fingertips and will be able to cope calmly with unexpected guests and unforeseen events which make shopping difficult.

IN THE LARDER

ALCOHOL: this is often the ingredient that transforms an ordinary dish into something special. Brandy, dry sherry, white wine, red wine, port, Grand Marnier, Kahlua and rum are useful, particularly in sauces.

ANCHOVIES: in jars or canned. Use for pizzas and pasta sauces.

BAKING POWDER: often a combination-bicarbonate of soda and cream of tartar.

CANNED FOOD: asparagus, bean sprouts, carrots, coconut milk, condensed milk, corn, crab meat, evaporated milk, fruit, mushrooms, potatoes, prawns, salmon, sardines, soups (asparagus, consomme, mushroom), tomatoes and tuna.

CEREALS: include bran for baking and wheatgerm for coating items such as fish fillets.

CHOCOLATE: dark and milk.

CHUTNEYS AND PICKLES: include capers, gherkins and olives.

DRIED AND GLACE FRUITS: include apples, apricots, cherries, raisins and sultanas.

FLOUR: plain and self-raising in both white and wholemeal. and cornflour.

FRUIT AND VEGETABLES: keep a selection of your family's favourites, including carrots, garlic, lemons, oranges, onions, potatoes and tomatoes.

GELATINE:

HERBS AND SPICES: keep an assortment of small quantities of dried herbs and spices (flavour fades with time) and try growing a few such as parsley, mint and basil to use fresh in salads, soups and as garnishes.

JAMS AND PRESERVES: include apricot jam for glazing, golden syrup and honey.

NUTS: include almonds, cashews and pinenuts. Buy in small quantities as they have a short shelf-life.

OILS: include peanut and olive.

PASTA AND NOODLES: a selection of different shapes.

PEANUT BUTTER: crunchy and smooth.

PEPPER: white and black.

RICE: include both brown and white long-grain; short-grain.

SALT: table and rock.

SAUCES: chilli, oyster, soy and tomato.

STOCK CUBES: include chicken and beef.

SUGAR: brown, white and icing.

VINEGARS: white wine and cider.

IN THE FREEZER

BACON: rewrap into convenient amounts between 4 to 6 slices.

BECHAMEL SAUCE: one of the most useful sauces you'll ever make. See recipe on page 14.

BERRY FRUITS: keep a variety. Can be used for sauces and for stirring through ice-cream or yoghurt for a quick, tasty dessert.

BREAD AND ROLLS: an assortment of shapes – white and wholemeal.

BUTTER: unsalted. Best stored in the freezer because it tends to go rancid more quickly than salted varieties that can be stored in the refrigerator.

CREPES: well worth going to the trouble to make up a batch. Stack them, separated by cling film or greaseproof paper and store them, wrapped, in the freezer for up to three months. Use for main courses and desserts with a variety of fillings.

ICE-CREAM.

PIZZA BASES: sold in packets of three.

SHEET PASTRY: buy ready-made puff, shortcrust and fillo.

SPINACH .

STOCKS: homemade beef, chicken and fish.

TOMATO SAUCE: homemade. Ideal as a sauce for pasta, or topping for pizza. See recipe on page 14.

IN THE REFRIGERATOR

BUTTER.

CHEESE: cheddar (grated) and parmesan. Keep a tub of ricotta (lasts about 1 week after opening) for use as a filling for lasagna or cannelloni. Mozzarella is useful for pizzas or as a topping for grilled chicken.

CREAM: thickened and light sour cream.

EGGS: keep a few at room temperature for baking.

YOGHURT: natural. Useful in curries and for quick desserts with fruit.

HYGIENE IN THE KITCHEN

Many government controls exist to ensure the food we buy, whether it be raw, canned, frozen or cooked, is prepared and stored as hygienically as possible – a dose of food poisoning is inconvenient, unpleasant and, at times, fatal. Bacteria are essential to life, and the vast majority cause no harm whatsoever. Others, if allowed to multiply in conditions they find favourable, can, and will, cause illness. Because we can't see them, we tend to forget they're there. From the moment you select food items in the supermarket or corner shop, the control over standards of hygiene is entirely in your hands. To serve safe food, always observe the basic rules of storage and handling.

TRANSPORTING FOOD

✎ Raw, frozen, partially or fully cooked foodstuffs must always be taken home as quickly as possible and stored in the freezer or refrigerator. Don't leave them in a car that is standing in the hot sun – seafood and dairy products, in particular, will deteriorate rapidly.
✎ Try to keep chilled food, such as a joint of raw meat, away from cooked food such as sliced ham. Cross-contamination can occur if the packaging is leaky and blood from the meat drips on to the ham.
✎ Don't put perishable foodstuffs in the boot of your car if any chemicals or strong-smelling items are stored there.

SAUCES, MARINADES AND DRESSINGS

A recipe doesn't have to be complicated to taste good. Here are some simple suggestions for dressing up plain food.

SAUCES
The following two sauces are probably the most useful you'll ever make. Store in containers of varying sizes so that you always have the correct amount to hand for use in whatever recipe you are preparing. Keep in the freezer for up to 3 months.

BECHAMEL SAUCE: don't take short-cuts making this creamy textured, subtly flavoured sauce – the time taken to make it properly results in a fine flavour. This quantity makes about 2½ cups.

2 cups of milk
1 medium onion, chopped
small piece of celery
1 carrot, halved
2 cloves
parsley or a bouquet garni
60g butter
60g plain flour
salt and pepper to taste

Place milk in a saucepan, bring slowly to the boil and add vegetables, cloves and parsley or bouquet garni. Leave over very low heat for about 30 minutes. This allows the milk to absorb the flavours of the other ingredients. Do not boil. Melt butter in a pan, stir in plain flour, stir over moderate heat for 2-3 minutes to make a roux. Don't allow to brown. Remove mixture from heat.

Strain the flavoured milk into a jug and discard vegetables and herbs. Gradually stir the milk into the roux, beating it with a whisk to avoid lumps forming. Return pan to heat, bring mixture to simmering point. Leave simmering very gently until it reaches the consistency of thickened cream; this may take an hour. Stir occasionally. Allow to cool. Store.

USES: pour over cooked vegetables (preferably crunchy ones), sprinkle with cheese, dot with butter and brown under the grill. This is also an excellent sauce for pouring over lasagna and other pasta shapes, moussaka and cooked, diced chicken.

Variations:
* Add 1 – 2 teaspoons Dijon mustard to the finished sauce.
* Add a handful of finely chopped parsley to the finished sauce.
* Cook 125g chopped mushrooms in a little butter. Stir through the finished sauce.
* Stir grated parmesan and nutmeg into the finished sauce.
* Add 1 cup Tomato Sauce (recipe follows) to sauce while it is hot. Reheat gently, stir in a little butter. Good with fish, chicken and egg dishes.

TOMATO SAUCE: homemade tomato sauce beats all others. Vary the quantity of onion, garlic and herbs to suit your own taste. Makes about 2 cups.

2 tablespoons olive oil
1 large onion, finely chopped
1 garlic clove, crushed
2 x 410g cans whole, peeled tomatoes
mixed herbs or fresh parsley, chopped
salt and black pepper
white wine to taste
1 tablespoon tomato paste

Heat olive oil in a frypan or large saucepan. Add chopped onion and crushed garlic. Saute over a moderate heat until soft and transparent; don't allow to brown. Add whole, peeled tomatoes in their juice. Break them up with a wooden spoon and combine with the mixture. Add a generous shake of mixed herbs (dried) or freshly chopped parsley. Season well with salt and freshly ground black pepper. Add a dash of white wine, if desired. Bring to the boil, cover and simmer for about 30 minutes – it should have a thick, pulpy consistency. Add tomato paste and adjust seasonings to taste. Cook a little longer to make sauce thicker, if desired. Allow to cool. Store.

USES: spread on pizza bases. Pour over pasta. Serve with barbecued meats. Use as a base for a fish casserole by adding a combination of white fish, green prawns, mussels and squid rings. Bake in a moderate oven for 30-40 minutes; or until fish is cooked through. Top with chopped parsley and cubed feta cheese. This sauce can also be made into a soup by thinning it with water or chicken stock – serve it chilled or hot.

Variations:
* Add some chopped carrot and celery with the tomatoes.
* Add a few drops of Tabasco in place of the herbs.
* Add freshly chopped coriander in place of the parsley. This has a strong flavour so don't add too much at once.

Speedy Sauces
* After pan-frying a pork chop or piece of chicken or beef, remove excess fat from the pan. Add a good dash of wine to the meat juices plus a dollop of cream; stir to combine all the crispy bits. Cook over a moderate heat for a few minutes. Pour over the meat.
* After pan-frying lamb chops, remove excess fat from pan, then add ¼ cup mint jelly. Stir until smooth and add ½ cup white wine. Bring to the boil. Add salt and pepper to taste, simmer a few minutes until thickened. Pour over meat.
* Combine equal quantities of tomato sauce (bottled or fresh), horseradish sauce and grainy mustard and spread over grilled fish fillets. Return to the grill and heat through.

* Place 1 stick of celery (strings removed), 125g blue-vein cheese, 1 clove of garlic, 1 tablespoon white wine vinegar and 1 shallot in the blender or food processor and process roughly. Add ½ cup cream and process till smooth. Pour into a bowl, sprinkle with paprika. Serve with barbecued meat.

* Place fruit and juice from a 425g can of berry fruit of your choice in a saucepan. Add ¾ cup brown sugar, bring to the boil, stirring until sugar has dissolved. Add ½ teaspoon cinnamon and boil, uncovered, for 10 minutes. Add 1 cup brandy and boil a further 5 minutes. Puree in the blender, then push through a fine sieve if a smoother consistency is desired. Store in the fridge in an airtight container. Serve over fresh fruit, ice-cream, mousses or sponge cake.

* Stir drained, tinned plums (stones removed) through thick natural yoghurt and chill well. Serve over plain sponge cake.

MARINADES

The process of marinating tenderises food and imparts a variety of flavours. Preparation for dishes that are marinated is mostly do-ahead, making them ideal for the busy cook. The marinade is poured over the meat or fish, covered, and left for at least an hour (always use a glass or ceramic dish as metal reacts to the acid in the marinade). Ideally, leave overnight for the maximum flavour to develop. Turn the meat or fish pieces occasionally. When you're ready to cook, just drain off the marinade and grill or barbecue the meat. Serve with a simple salad.

FOR LAMB AND VEAL CUTLETS

2½ cm piece ginger, grated
1 leek, thinly sliced
1 cup green ginger wine
1 clove garlic, crushed
rind (grated) and juice of one lime

Combine ingredients and pour over lamb or veal cutlets.

FOR PORK CHOPS

½ cup peanut oil
¼ cup cider vinegar
¼ cup brandy
¼ teaspoon ground cumin
1 tablespoon honey
1 tablespoon black pepper

Combine ingredients and pour over pork chops.

FOR KEBABS

1 medium onion, chopped
2 tablespoons ground ginger
1 teaspoon ground turmeric
1 teaspoon garam masala
¼ teaspoon ground nutmeg
200g plain natural yoghurt

Combine onion, ginger, turmeric, garam masala and nutmeg in a blender or food processor. Stir through cubed lamb or beef. Add yoghurt and stir through the meat to coat thoroughly. After marinating, thread on skewers, and grill or barbecue.

FOR SEAFOOD

1 cup dry white wine
½ cup fresh lemon juice
2 tablespoons white wine vinegar
2 tablespoons olive oil
salt and black pepper to taste

Combine ingredients and pour mixture over pieces of firm white fish, green prawns, calamari rings and scallops, making sure they are coated thoroughly. Cover and leave overnight in the fridge. Drain the seafood and serve. The marinade has the effect of "cooking" the fish so that no further preparation is needed. As an alternative, try a combination of the juice of 2 limes and ½ cup coconut milk (available in cans from supermarkets).

DRESSINGS

With the great increases in vegetable varieties now available to us, salads have become colourful, flavoursome feasts. An interesting dressing tops the whole meal off perfectly.

ORANGE DRESSING

1 teaspoon wholegrain mustard
1 teaspoon soft brown sugar
2 tablespoons grapeseed oil
rind of 1 small orange, grated
1 tablespoon orange juice
2 tablespoons white wine vinegar or tarragon vinegar

Serving suggestion: combine ingredients and serve over salad.

SALAD DRESSING

2 tablespoons lemon juice
3 tablespoons peanut oil
3 garlic cloves, crushed
salt and pepper to taste

Serving suggestion: combine ingredients and serve over fresh tomatoes and fennel.

SWEET MUSTARD DRESSING

4 tablespoons olive oil
1 tablespoon Dijon mustard
2 tablespoons honey
2 tablespoons white wine vinegar
salt and pepper to taste

Serving suggestion: combine ingredients and pour over a mixture of two or three types of lettuce and cubes of blue-vein or Cheshire-type cheese.

YOGHURT DRESSING

6 tablespoons olive oil
2 tablespoons thick natural yoghurt
2 tablespoons cider vinegar
1 tablespoon honey
salt and black pepper to taste

Serving suggestion: combine ingredients and pour over a salad of yellow, red and green capsicum, cucumber and witloof. Top with a little chopped coriander.

SOUR CREAM DRESSING

1 carton of light, sour cream
salt and pepper to taste
lemon juice

Serving suggestion: season sour cream with salt and pepper. Add a squeeze of lemon juice. Serve with sliced avocados and diced crisp green apples. Sprinkle pinenuts or sesame seeds over the top.

CITRUS DRESSING

rind (grated) and juice of 1 orange
1 tablespoon lemon juice
4 tablespoons peanut oil
salt and pepper to taste

Serving suggestion: combine ingredients and season with salt and pepper. Mix through hot new potatoes and sprinkle with chopped chives or shallots.

SESAME DRESSING

1 clove garlic, chopped
2½cm piece of ginger
Tabasco for flavour
1 teaspoon brown sugar
2 tablespoons white wine vinegar
3 tablespoons water
2 teaspoons soy sauce
1 teaspoon sesame oil

Serving suggestion: put garlic, ginger, a few drops of Tabasco, brown sugar, white wine vinegar, water and soy sauce in a pan. Stir over medium heat until sugar dissolves. Bring to the boil. Remove from heat; strain. Add sesame oil. Cool. Serve over lightly steamed, crunchy vegetables.

POPPY SEED DRESSING

3 tablespoons sunflower oil
1 teaspoon lemon juice
1 tablespoon poppy seeds
salt and pepper to taste

Serving suggestion: combine ingredients and pour over cubed blue-vein cheese and slices of ripe pear. Garnish with mint leaves.

COCKTAIL PARTIES

Many people's idea of cocktail food is something that is impossible to handle unless you have two pairs of hands and/or a knife and fork. Cocktail food must be finger food – one hand is required to hold a glass, the other to hold the food. Keep it simple.

☞ Avoid greasy items or anything that will stain (such as beetroot). Your guests won't thank you if they have a permanent reminder of the party on their clothes.

☞ Choose only one or two items that require assembling at the last minute.

☞ Add fillings to pastry cases at the last minute to avoid cases becoming soggy.

☞ Allow about 500g ice cubes per person.

☞ If you have more bottles of wine to chill than you can fit in your refrigerator, draw the corks slightly and layer the bottles with ice in a clean plastic garbage bin.

BUFFET DINNER FOR A CROWD

☞ Disposable plates are acceptable because they come in very durable materials and attractive designs. However, disposable cutlery is neither attractive nor useful – it is frequently so flimsy that it won't cut properly.

Hire cutlery and glasses from a catering firm.

☞ Disposable napkins are useful, but stick to white, thick-ply ones. The thinner ones disintegrate very easily, while the patterned ones can, if they get wet, transfer their cheerful colours to people's clothes.

☞ Supply plenty of soft, non-fizzy drinks.

☞ Have several bottle openers handy – they have an extraordinary knack of disappearing just when you need one.

DINNER PARTIES

☞ Don't be one of those hosts or hostesses who spends most of the time in the kitchen rather than with the guests. Last-minute preparation is inevitable on some items, but try to plan a menu that is as much do-ahead as possible. If you make a step-by-step plan of action, you can start preparations as much as two or three days ahead.

☞ Don't attempt something complicated that you have never cooked before. If you are trying to impress, it is better to prepare a tried and tested recipe you know will work. Save experimenting for when you have some spare time.

☞ Keep a record of the menus you have served your friends so that you don't serve them the same thing next time they come. You'll soon forget who ate what unless you jot it down.

Supermarkets and delicatessens stock an intriguing array of ingredients from all over the world. In fact more and more are arriving as we become increasingly interested in the cuisines of other countries. This short check list will help you identify some items. Buy them and try them in your own cooking. Many of the ingredients listed here are not unique to one country's cuisine.

ITALY

1. BOCCONCINI: small rounds of very fresh mozzarella cheese. Use within a couple of days. Try cutting into slivers and serving with slices of ripe tomato. Garnish with chopped basil.

2. COPPA: cured pork shoulders.

3. MASCARPONE: a cheese with the consistency of heavy cream. Short shelf life. Sold in tubs. A good accompaniment to fruit such as figs.

4. PASTA: available fresh and dried in many different shapes.

5. PESTO: a sauce made from fresh basil leaves, pinenuts and oil. Can be bought ready-made in jars. Serve over pasta.

6. POMODORI SECCHI: sun-dried tomatoes preserved in olive oil. Intense tomato flavour. Use in sauces or serve as part of an antipasto platter.

7. PORCINI: flavoursome brown mushroom. Available dried for use in sauces.

SPAIN AND PORTUGAL

1. BACALAO (Spanish)

1. BACALHAU (Portuguese): salted cod. Soak in several changes of water for 24 hours. Grill or fry.

2. CHORIZO (Spanish):

2. CHOURICO (Portuguese): smoked sausage usually made from pork offcuts, herbs and spices. Serve grilled. Can be removed from skins and used in casseroles.

3. QUINCE PASTE: rich and fruity, this is eaten with bread and cheese.

4. SAFFRON: comes from the stigmas of the saffron crocus. Essential in paella. Real saffron has no substitute and is very expensive. Coloured powders are available to give food a similar golden colour, but they are a poor alternative.

5. SUNFLOWER SEEDS: called pipes in Spain. Serve as a snack or in casseroles.

INDIA

1. CARDAMOM: available in pod, seed or powdered form.

2. CHILLIES: available fresh, dried or ground. Many types and sizes are available; the small ones are the hottest.

3. CURRY LEAVES: available fresh or dried. Similar appearance to bay leaves. Imparts a mild curry taste.

4. FENUGREEK: available as dried seeds. Used in curries, pickles and chutneys.

5, 6 & 7. FLOUR: ata (5) a fine whole-wheat flour. Besan (6) made from ground chick peas, is used as a thickening agent and as an ingredient in pastry, batters, pancakes and various other dishes. Rice flour (7) is used in sweets where it functions like a cornflour, and in pancakes and chapatis.

8. GARAM MASALA: a condiment made from several spices. It may include cardamom, cinnamon, cloves, fennel seed, cumin or any one of about 16 spices. The final taste and aroma is very much up to personal choice. Garam masala can be bought ready-made in jars and packets.

9. GHEE: clarified butter in which the water and any impurities have been driven off by heating. Available in tins and tubs.

10. TAMARIND: the pulp around the seeds of the tamarind tree is used for its fruity, sour taste. The pulp is soaked in hot water and allowed to cool. The pulp is then squeezed thoroughly and the resultant flavoured water is used in cooking.

CHINA

1. BEAN CURD: a curd made from soy beans. Comes in a variety of textures, colours and shapes. Similar to Japanese tofu. Used in vegetables, soups and stir-fried dishes. Has little taste of its own but marries well with other ingredients.

2.. BOK CHOY: one of the choy family of vegetables, resembling cabbage or spinach. Both leaf and stalk can be used in stir-fried dishes, or steamed.

3. CELLOPHANE NOODLES: made from mung bean starch paste, these fine, transparent noodles can be soaked, then fried or boiled. Can also be fried straight from the packet.

4. FIVE SPICE POWDER: a mixture of star anise, fennel, cinnamon, cloves and Szechwan pepper.

5. HOI SIN SAUCE: spicy sweet sauce made from soy beans and spices. Good with pork dishes.

6. MUSHROOMS: There are numerous varieties of which oyster and straw are just two of the best known. Available dried and fresh. Dried mushrooms must be soaked in water for about 30 minutes before use. Discard stalks. Intense flavour, so only a few need be used.

7. OYSTER SAUCE: made from oysters cooked in salted soy sauce.

8. PLUM SAUCE: a spicy/sweet sauce made from chillies, plums, vinegar and spices. Serve with meat.

9 & 10. SOY SAUCE: many varieties avaliable.The light soy sauce (9) is a thin sauce generally used for flavouring. The dark, thick sauce (10) is used primarily as a colouring agent.

11. STAR ANISE: star-shaped, this is the dried fruit of a Chinese evergreen of the same name. Has a pungent, licorice taste.

12. RED BEAN PASTE: a sweet bean paste made from soy beans and sugar. White bean paste is made from lotus seed. Used as a filling for Chinese pastries.

13. WONTON WRAPPERS: squares of fresh noodle dough used for making dim sum (a variety of steamed or fried morsels filled with meat, fish or sweet ingredients). Found in the freezer at Chinese supermarkets.

SOUTH–EAST ASIA

1 & 2. GALANGAL: a relation of ginger. Available fresh (1) and dried (2).

3. KAFFIR LIME: has a more intense flavour than the regular lime. Both skin and leaves are used. Available dry or in brine.

4. KEMIRI NUTS: also known as candle nuts. Toxic in their raw state, they are always sold roasted. They are ground and used to thicken Malay and Indonesian curries.

5. KRUPUK: crackers made from prawn, fish, potatoes or rice. Fry in oil.

6 & 7. LEMON GRASS: available fresh and dried. Has an intense lemon taste.

8. PALM SUGAR: produced from the sap of coconut and palmyra palms. A dark sugar sold in round, flat cakes.

9. SAMBAL DJEROEK: made from lemon juice and Indonesian sour fruits.

10. SAMBAL OELEK: paste made from ground chillies and salt.

11. SHRIMP PASTE: strong flavoured dark brown paste made from salted dried shrimp.

12. NAM PLA: a fish sauce used in Thai cooking. (Known as nuoc mam in Vietnam.) Made from liquid fermented from salted fish.

MIDDLE EAST

1. BURGHUL: hulled wheat, ground to various degrees of fineness. Has a nutty taste. Soak in water to soften. Used in kibbeh and tabbouleh.

2. CHICK PEAS: also known as garbanzos. Available mostly in dried form. Cover with water and leave overnight. Drain, cover with fresh water and boil until tender. Used with tahini (see right) as the base of the popular dip hummus.

3. FETA: Greek in origin. A soft, crumbly, slightly salty cheese.

4. HALOUMI: salty, stringy cheese. Can be fried and served with lemon juice.

5. HALVA: a sweet made from sweetened sesame seed paste, containing almonds or pistachios.

6. LABAN: Lebanese for yoghurt or cultured milk.

7 & 8. MAHAWAR: rosewater, used in savoury and sweet dishes. Mazahar (8) is orange flower water.

9. OKRA: pod-shaped vegetable, also known as ladies' fingers or gumbo. Usually fried before being cooked with meat and other ingredients.

10. PASTOURMA: dried beef with a highly spiced, thick coating that usually includes paprika and chilli pepper. Slice thinly and eat with bread.

11. TAHINI: a paste made from toasted sesame seeds. Available in jars.

JAPAN

1. BONITO: dried fish used as a flavouring for soups and stocks.

2. DAIKON: also known as mooli, this is a large, mildly flavoured radish.

3 & 4. DASHI: a broth made from dried bonito and kombu (4), a type of seaweed.

5. LOTUS ROOT: a creamy white, decorative vegetable used in Chinese and Japanese cooking. Available in tins.

6. MIRIN: Japanese rice wine used only in cooking.

7. MISO: paste made from cooked, fermented soy beans. Salty taste.

8. NORI: dried seaweed. Sold in thin sheets. Must be toasted before use.

9. SAKE: rice wine served as a drink but can also be used in cooking.

10. SHIITAKE: a variety of mushroom. It is available dried.

11. SHOYU: Japanese soy sauce.

12. TAMARI: a soy bean product, it is used as a dipping sauce.

13. TOFU: a bland soy bean product similar to bean curd (see China).

14. WASABI: a very pungent green horseradish. Sold in tubes and tins. Use as an accompaniment to raw fish dishes.

30 FREEZER SHORTCUTS

1. Use ice-cube trays to freeze small quantities of food, for example stock, soup, fruit juice, sauces, baby food. After freezing transfer to plastic bags for convenient use.

2. Freeze fruit, for example strawberries, grapes and cherries in the centre of plain ice-cubes, for decorative effect in drinks and punches.

3. Store jams and preserves in the freezer to prevent them becoming mouldy during humid weather.

4. Freeze ground coffee and coffee beans to retain their flavour longer.

5. Spoon soft biscuit mixtures onto a tray, and freeze. When frozen, lift off with a spatula, pack and seal.

6. Leftover piping cream can be piped in rosettes then frozen. These rosettes can be served with hot and cold drinks for a decorative effect.

7. Store nuts, seeds and coconut in the freezer to keep them fresh longer.

8. An easy way to slice meat thinly is to partially freeze the whole piece of meat until firm. Using a sharp knife, cut meat into thin slices.

9. Stale bread and cake can be crumbed and frozen for later use.

10. Leftover cheese can be grated and frozen to use at a later date. For example, as pizza topping.

11. Keep a container filled with butter balls or curls ready for entertaining.

12. Butchers paper, cellophane and waxed paper are not recommended to use when freezing. These materials are not moisture or vapour proof and deterioration of the food will result if they are used.

13. Small cuts of steak and chops are best packaged and frozen in a single layer.

14. Freezing small food items on an open tray for an hour or so before packaging enables small portions to be removed from the bag or container and the remainder returned to the freezer.

15. Decorated cakes and tarts should be frozen before packaging to prevent icing being damaged.

INTERNATIONAL FOOD TERMS

Australian	American	British
125g butter	1 stick of butter	4oz butter(¼ pound)
baking trays	cookie sheets	baking trays
bicarbonate of soda	baking soda	bicarbonate of soda
black-eyed beans	black-eyed peas	black-eyed beans
broad beans	fava beans	broad beans
butter lettuce	butterhead lettuce	cabbage lettuce
capsicum	sweet or bell pepper	green or red pepper
castor sugar	superfine sugar	caster sugar
chick peas	garbanzo beans	chick peas
chillies	hot peppers	chillies
chokos	chayote	chayota
(to) chop	mince	(to) chop
coriander	Chinese parsley	coriander
corned beef	salt beef	corned beef
cornflour	cornstarch	cornflour
cos lettuce	Romaine lettuce	Cos or Romaine lettuce
cream	light cream	single cream
cube sugar	loaf sugar	cube or lump sugar
essence	extract	essence
eggplant	eggplant or aubergine	aubergine
endive	escerole or chicory	endive
fillet (of meat)	tenderloin	fillet
firmly beaten egg whites	dry egg whites	firmly beaten egg whites
fried	pan-broiled or pan fried	fried
frying pan	skillet	frying pan
glace fruit	candied fruit	glace fruit
gravy beef	stew beef	gravy beef
grill, griller	broil, broiler	grill, griller
ground rice, rice flour	rice flour	ground rice
hard-boiled egg	hard cooked egg	hard-boiled egg

stralian	American	British
g sugar	confectioners' sugar	icing sugar, powdered sugar
	conserve	jam, conserve
g prawns	jumbo shrimps	shrimps
ce/minced meat	ground (meat)	mince/minced (meat)
ello or sour cherries	sour cherries	morello cherries
rtadella	baloney	mortadella
l	variety meat	offal
a	ladies' fingers or gumbo	okra
paw, pawpaw	papaya	pawpaw
mientos	pimientos	pimentos
n flour	all-purpose flour	plain flour
ato flour	potato starch	potato flour
wns	shrimps	shrimps
rub butter or fat into ingredients	cut in shortening	(to) rub butter or fat into dry ingredients
molina	farina	semolina
ame seeds	benne seeds	sesame seeds
llots, spring onions	scallions, green onions	spring onions
shell	(to) shuck or hull	(to) shell
rtcrust pastry	basic pastry or shortcrust pastry	shortcrust
w peas	sugar snap peas	mange tout
r cream	dairy sour cream	soured cream
ck cubes	bouillon cubes	stock cubes
anas	seedless white raisins or golden raisins	white raisins or sultanas
ets thermometer	jellmeter	jam or candy thermometer
iss roll pan	jelly-roll pan	Swiss roll pan
ckened cream	heavy cream	double cream
salted butter	sweet butter	unsalted butter
cchini	zucchini	courgette

16. Add a pinch of ascorbic acid to the cold sugar syrup when preparing fruits, for example apricots and peaches for freezing to prevent fruit discolouring.

17. Most leftover canned foods can be frozen with the liquid from the can. Thaw at room temperature for about 1 hour and drain before using.

18. When making biscuits, double the quantity, freeze ½ quantity for later use.

19. Always keep 1 to 2 loaves of bread in the freezer for emergency use.

20. Freeze orange wedges to serve as a healthy ice-block to children.

21. Freeze leftover egg whites and egg yolks for later use.

22. Store unfilled baked flan cases in the freezer for emergency meals.

23. Freeze water in loaf pans or cake pans. When frozen, remove "bricks" from pans and wrap in foil. Use these ice "bricks" to keep drinks cold for parties. They will stay cold and solid for hours if kept wrapped in foil.

24. Freeze left over tea and coffee in ice-cube trays to serve with iced coffee or tea, without diluting the flavour.

25. Freeze lemon, lime and orange slices to have on hand during summer months. These can be served in drinks.

26. Try to shape packages for freezing in easy, convenient shapes. Line ice-cream containers with large freezer bags, place contents in containers, freeze, then remove from container for easy stacking.

27. Small quantities of roux made from butter and plain flour can be frozen to thicken hot liquids during cooking. Freeze in 1 tablespoon portions, stir frozen roux into saucepan to thicken hot liquid.

28. Leftover fruit juices and syrups from canned fruit can be frozen in ice-cube trays and used for preparing sweet sauces or for serving with fruit salads.

29. Leftover fresh yeast can be frozen. A frozen cube of yeast will be ready for use after 30 minutes.

30. Freeze leftover sweet and savoury foods to create lunch boxes that cater for individual tastes. This will save time when family members are leaving at different times in the morning.

MAKING USE OF A FREEZER

✏ Before freezing food, turn the control switch to the lowest setting or switch on the freezing control.

✏ Freeze only foods that are in perfect, fresh condition.

✏ Handle food as little as possible and keep it clean.

✏ Foil punctures easily, so overwrap with heavy-duty polythene.

✏ Introduce fresh food gradually – no more than one tenth of the freezer's capacity a day.

✏ The length of time for food to become frozen varies according to the type of food and the size and density of the packages; it is best to leave all foods overnight.

✏ Once the food is solidly frozen, stack it tightly in the storage zone ready for the next batch of food.

✏ Cool hot food for freezing quickly; put in a cool part of the kitchen or stand container in a basin of cold water.

✏ DON'T put warm foods in the freezer; it creates condensation.

✏ Seal the food in moisture and vapour proof materials or the food will go grey and lose its flavour. Wrap so that all air is excluded, otherwise the food can suffer "freezer burn".

✏ When freezing liquids, leave 1cm space at the top of the container to allow for expansion of the liquid.

✏ Thickened and semi-liquid foods become thicker as a result of freezing, so make them a bit runnier than usual. If they separate, you can usually cure this by beating well during reheating.

✏ Seal plastic bags with pegs – each colour indicating a different type of food.

✏ Keep a list of food and packing dates on inside of freezer door or lid.

DO NOT FREEZE

✏ Fresh milk will separate and will not reconstitute.

✏ Hard-boiled eggs become very leathery if frozen.

✏ Yoghurt, sour cream and mayonnaise separate when frozen.

✏ Don't freeze highly seasoned foods, the flavourings alter or intensify during storage.

✏ Never store carbonated drinks in the freezer; they can explode.

✏ Pasta loses its texture if frozen.

✏ Be wary of freezing fish and shellfish; it has often been frozen during transportation.

✏ Never refreeze anything.

Food will remain in good condition for at least eight hours in the event of a power cut or breakdown. Don't open the freezer to see how the food is faring; it takes 12-14 hours for food in an unopened freezer to thaw out.

If food has thawed, DO NOT refreeze it.

DEFROSTING YOUR FREEZER

✏ Defrost when food stocks are low, for example, after the school holidays, or towards the end of the winter. It should only be necessary to defrost once a year.

1. Switch off and unplug the freezer.

2. Remove food and wrap it up in thick layers of newspaper, blankets or a doona.

3. Allow ice to melt, then wipe up water with towels. Don't scrape the icy bits with anything sharp or you will damage the freezer lining. Wipe out the inside with warm water and bicarbonate of soda.

4. Switch the power on, turn the freezer to its lowest setting and leave it closed for an hour before returning the food.

30 MICROWAVE SHORTCUTS

1. An easy way to open fresh mussels and oysters is to place 6 to 8 mussels or oysters around the microwave turntable and microwave on HIGH for 30 to 40 seconds. Discard any unopened shells.

2. To make cutting and peeling pumpkin easier, microwave the pumpkin on HIGH for about 2 minutes.

3. To easily remove the skin from garlic, microwave on HIGH, allow about 30 seconds per clove.

4. You can ripen avocadoes in the microwave by microwaving on LOW for up to 2 minutes, turning the avocado once during cooking. Be careful not to over heat the avocado as it will blacken inside.

5. Always reheat rice with one tablespoon of water, stock, wine or a knob of butter to prevent drying out.

6. Fresh herbs can be dried in the microwave by placing a single layer of herbs between 2 pieces of paper towelling and microwaving on HIGH for 2 minutes. Stand for 1 minute. Repeat process until the herbs are dry. The time will vary with the type of herb.

7. To make crisp pork crackling, carve the cooked crackling into serving size pieces and place between paper towels. Microwave on HIGH for 2 minutes at a time until the crackling hardens.

8. To make bottled sauce easier to pour, remove lid, microwave on HIGH for about 20 seconds.

9. To liquefy crystallised honey, remove lid, microwave on HIGH for about 30 seconds.

10. To toast coconut, scatter 1 cup onto a large microwave safe plate, microwave on HIGH for about 4 minutes, stirring several times during cooking. Be careful it does not burn.

11. If in doubt about the suitability of a plate or dish for use in a microwave oven, stand the dish in the oven with a glass of water next to it. Microwave on HIGH for 1 minute. If the dish remains cold it is microwave safe. If it gets hot, don't use it in the microwave oven.

12. To wilt a bunch of spinach for use in pies etc., wash spinach, remove stems, cut spinach. Place spinach in a microwave-safe dish and microwave on HIGH for 1 to 2 minutes.

13. To eliminate soaking dried beans and pulses overnight, place beans in microwave-safe bowl, cover with water, bring to boil on HIGH for about 10 minutes, then simmer on DEFROST for 30 to 40 minutes.

14. Warming cheese in the microwave before serving brings out its full flavour. Microwave 250g tasty cheese on LOW for about 45 seconds, stand 5 minutes. Microwave 250g camembert or brie on LOW for about 30 seconds, stand 5 minutes.

15. Citrus fruit will produce more juice if it is heated on HIGH for about 30 seconds per fruit. Allow the fruit to stand before squeezing it.

16. When melting chocolate, it will not appear melted, test by stirring before adding extra cooking time.

17. To soften hard ice-cream, microwave on LOW for about 20 seconds at a time, to make it easier to scoop.

18. Toast nuts and dried seeds on HIGH in a single layer in a shallow microwave safe plate. Allow 5 minutes per 100g, stirring during cooking.

19. Use castor sugar when cooking in the microwave, its fine texture will dissolve quicker.

20. Covering foods in the microwave shortens the cooking time and retains the moisture in the food.

21. Stale biscuits and crackers can be crisped in the microwave. Spread biscuits or crackers in a single layer, microwave on HIGH for about 20 seconds, stand a few minutes.

Pappadums can be cooked in the
wave. Place 4 pappadums around
the turntable, microwave on HIGH
out 4 minutes, turn after 2 minutes.

To peel tomatoes, peaches etc.
the skin lightly with a fork, microwave
GH for about 1 minute per item.
5 minutes before peeling.

When cooking fish fillets, overlap the
il ends for even cooking.

To reconstitute dried fruit, add 1 to 3
spoons water, wine or fruit juice for
cup of fruit, cover and microwave on
for about 1 to 2 minutes, stir well.

Strong or stale odours can be
ved from the oven interior by washing
ith vinegar, lemon or vanilla flavoured
, or heating 2 cups water containing 2
lices lemon on HIGH for about 8
es, then wipe the oven immediately.

When using paper towels or napkins
absorbent base or covering for foods
microwave, ensure that they are
as dyes may run from coloured
rs and stain the food.

To prevent food from drying out
reheating in the microwave oven,
le or spray a fine mist of water onto
ce of food before covering.

To dry fresh breadcrumbs, scatter 2
of crumbs over a paper towel lined,
wave safe plate, microwave on
for about 2 to 3 minutes, stir crumbs
g cooking, cool, before storing.

Cook bacon rashers between
s of paper towels as this will absorb
t, prevent splattering and keep oven
clean. Cook on HIGH for about 1
e per slice.

ROWAVE TIPS
DO NOT use metal dishes or dishes
metal trim or handles, or fine crystal
s in the microwave. Metal disturbs the
etic field and causes sparks.
Plastic storage and icecream containers
e used for reheating some food as long
s not too high in butter, oil, sugar or
y content. The food, when hot, will dis-
r melt the plastic.
Don't use dishes that have been
red with glue, the glue will melt.
Use aluminium foil to cover thinner parts
d (end of chicken drumsticks or wings)
rners of rectangular dishes where food
s first. The foil reflects the waves and
the cooked food from drying out.
Oven bags are good to use in the
wave. Do not secure them with paper,

plastic or foil-covered metal tags, use a rubber band or string.

✏ For even cooking, buy fish, chicken and
vegetables of similar size and thickness.
Chop meat and vegetables evenly.

✏ Don't boil eggs.

✏ Pierce membranes of food with skewer
or fork (eggs; white and yolk, potatoes and
tomatoes etc.).

✏ The golden rule for cooking successfully
in microwaves is to undercook, check the
food, then cook in short bursts.

✏ It is necessary to stir food or rearrange
dishes in the microwave so as to allow the
food to cook more evenly.

More and more of our winemakers are using
varietal labelling, calling the wine by the
grape variety or varieties from which it was
made. Of course, different winemakers,
using the same grape varieties, will end up
with dissimilar wines, just as two cooks,
using identical ingredients but different techniques, will produce disparate dishes. The
only way to find out exactly what is in the
bottle is to try the wine, but, as a rough guide:

WHITE VARIETAL WINES

CHARDONNAY has been the boom grape
of the 1980s. Everyone enjoys its fullbodied,
fruity flavour. It's an easy drinking wine which
goes with almost any food, from soup and
pasta to cheese and fruit.

SEMILLION is the great white grape of the
Hunter Valley of NSW, and is widely grown in
other regions. Crisp, dry semillion, in its
youth, complements luncheon dishes and
summer salads. Aged Hunter whites have
the character to go with rich poultry dishes
and mature cheese.

SAUVIGNON BLANC has a bouquet of
freshly cut grass, and a strong, grapey
flavour. Try it with fish and shellfish dishes,

TRAMINER (or Gewurtztraminer) has a
bouquet of rose petals and a powerful flavour
which is luscious without being sweet. It is an
excellent wine with spicy oriental food.

RHINE RIESLING is Australia's best sell-
ing varietal white wine. It has a delicate
aroma and a fresh fruit flavour when young,
and develops complexity with age. Young
riesling is an excellent aperitif, and an ideal
partner for fish, salads and pasta.

SWEET WHITE WINES are often labelled
Late Picked, Spatlese or Auslese, and are
generally made from Riesling or Semillion.
Don't restrict them to the sweets course: try
them with rich lobster or crab dishes, or with
fruit and blue vein cheese.

RED VARIETAL WINES

CABERNET SAUVIGNON is used to make
some of the world's best wines; our own
Coonawarra Cabernets amongst them. It's a

stylish wine, with a bouquet and flavour of
blackberries or plums, Enjoy it with red
meats, but especially with roast lamb.

MERLOT has a rich, meaty quality, which
is why it is usually blended with Cabernet to
make a softer, even fruitier red. Excellent
with veal and pork.

PINOT NOIR is a light to medium bodied
red with a raspberry bouquet and a soft
chocolate flavour. Drink with roast chicken,
and oriental dishes of pork and crabmeat.

SHIRAZ is the most widely planted red
grape in Australia, and some magnificent
wines are made from this variety. Its qualities
include a spicy, peppery flavour and a soft,
warm finish. Shiraz is the perfect complement for winter casseroles, stews and roasts
of beef and pork.

STORAGE

✏ All wines are better if "rested" before
they are drunk. Try to buy wine about two
days before you wish to drink it.

✏ Store wine in a dark area as light can
cause deterioration of the wine. If possible,
the storage area should remain around the
same temperature at all times and be kept
free of draughts.

✏ Table wines that are to be stored for a
long time should be stacked horizontally,
preferably on racks, so that the corks are
kept moist and expanded. Port, sherry and
other fortified wines can be stored upright.

SERVING WINE

✏ Red wine is best served at room
temperature. Stand the bottle in a warm part
of the room and open it a few hours before
you intend to drink it to allow it to breathe. If
you prefer you can decant the wine. Pour
wine slowly and carefully into selected
decanter (it should already be at room
temperature) until sediment begins to flow.

✏ If you are unable to get a cork out of a
bottle completely, strain the wine through a
clean tea strainer. This will get rid of the cork
pieces that remain.

✏ Don't open sparkling wines or cham-
pagne until you are ready to serve them; they
go flat.

✏ Before serving, wipe the mouth of the
bottle with a clean cloth.

COOKING WITH WINE

Wine has many uses in cooking.

✏ To improve the flavour of a sauce, add
a dash of red or white wine.

✏ To tenderise and enrich meat, marinade
it for 12 hours in wine before cooking. Use
equal quantities of wine and water as stock
in stews and casseroles. Baste roasts with
wine as they cook.

✏ When wine is served with food, it
remains active and retains its individuality;
flavours may contrast or complement the
dish. When wine is an ingredient, poured in
during cooking, the union of flavours
enhances the final result.

FOOD FACTS

EAT LIMITED AMOUNTS OF THIS GROUP
(fats, oils, sugar, salt)

EAT MODERATE AMOUNTS OF THIS GROUP
(dairy products, eggs, lean meats, nuts, legumes)

EAT THE MOST FROM THIS GROUP
(bread, cereals, fruit and vegetables)

Good eating habits, unfortunately, do not come naturally to everyone. Our diets frequently contain too much salt, sugar and fat, and not enough fruit and vegetables and fibre; often we're not even sure what is in the food we are eating. Here, we have outlined the major food groups, listed their nutritional value, given tips on storage and included a food additives chart to help you work out what those numbers on labels mean - sure to be a bonus for anyone suffering from an allergy. There is also a list of vitamins and minerals on page 53 which explains their importance in your eating plan. We haven't forgotten the basics however, we show you the different cuts of meat and how to cook them, how to carve meat, to cut up a chicken, to shell a prawn and to fillet a fish with a minimum of fuss.

In nutritional terms, the seven cereals – barley, maize, millet, oats, rice, rye, wheat – are fairly similar. They provide a range of nutrients rather than being rich sources of any one nutrient. The milling of cereals for flour removes some of the bran and germ which contain a proportion of the grain's vitamins, minerals and dietary fibre. When rice is polished, all the bran and germ are removed.

NUTRIENTS SUPPLIED BY CEREALS

Calcium, complex carbohydrates, iron, protein, B-Group Vitamins, Vitamin E and small amounts of phosphorous, potassium, magnesium, manganese, copper and zinc are found in cereals. The fat content of cereals is very low, with the exception of oats.

Cereal proteins have suffered a poor reputation because of the low proportion of essential amino acids, particularly lysine. However, most civilisations have developed traditional food patterns based on a staple cereal, supplemented with small quantities of fish, dairy products, meat, nuts or legumes. Interestingly, the protein content of wheat is considerably higher, on average, than that of other cereals.

THE GRAINS AND THEIR USES

BARLEY: mainly used for animal feed and for malting. Malted grain is important in the brewing and baking industries. As a food barley is eaten as a meal or flour, as barley groats and flakes and as pearl barley for thickening.

MAIZE: used to make corn bread, tortillas, breakfast cereal, popcorn, puffed snack foods and animal feed, or eaten as a vegetable (corn-on-the-cob).

MILLET: white-grains are preferred for eating while the red-grains are mainly used for making beer. In some countries millet and sorghum seeds are pounded into flour.

OATS: human consumption is small as the husk surrounding the grain must be removed to make it digestible. Oats are eaten as oatmeal and rolled oats – well-known as porridge and muesli. Oatcakes are popular in Scotland and Ireland.

RICE: rice grains are usually polished before being used for steaming or boiling. Used also for breakfast cereals, Japanese sake and Chinese rice wine.

RYE: rye is the only cereal besides wheat which can be baked into bread. Used also for crispbreads and in the liquor industry to make whisky, gin and beer.

WHEAT: is most important as a human food source. Used to make bread, breakfast cereals (puffed, shredded, flaked or compressed), baked products (cakes, biscuits, pastries, noodles, pasta), wheat germ (a rich source of Vitamin E) and bran.

BREAD

All types of bread – eg. white, mixed grain, wholemeal – supply a significant proportion of energy, protein and B-Group Vitamins. Bread also supplies calcium, phosphorous and iron but is NOT a good source of vitamins A, D or C. Bread is low in fat and contains minimal sugar, the extra fat comes in the form of spreads and toppings. Both wholemeal and white bread form part of a nutritious diet and each has advantages. Eating a mixture of different breads (rather than one) is recommended on nutritional grounds. As a source of fibre, wholemeal bread supplies more than white – almost twice that of mixed grain bread and two and a half times that of white bread.

Varieties of bread

BROWN: contains at least 50 percent wholemeal flour and has a dietary fibre content between wholemeal and white.

FIBRE-INCREASED WHITE: usually provides same fibre content as wholemeal bread, and is generally protein increased.

KIBBLED WHEAT, CRUSHED WHEATEN AND CRACKED WHEAT: may contain or be rolled in kibbled (cracked) wheat grains. Its nutritional value is similar to brown bread.

LEBANESE/PITA: made from white and/or wholemeal flour, yeast, salt and water. Not suitable for yeast-free diets.

LOW-SALT: contains 75 percent less salt with a maximum of 120mg sodium to 100g bread. Some breads use potassium chloride as a replacement for salt.

MIXED-GRAIN: made from a mixture of wholemeal and white flour, rye meal and flour. May contain wheat germ, honey, gluten, non-fat milk solids, cracked and other whole grains. Its nutritional value is similar to brown bread.

RYE: must contain at least 30 percent rye flour or meal. Dark rye has a higher proportion of rye flour, whole rye or rye meal. Traditionally, dark rye and pumpernickel are not made with yeast but with sour dough.

SALT-REDUCED: has 33 percent less salt; salt content must not exceed 345mg per 100g bread.

SOYA/POTATO/RICE: contains approximately 10 percent soya, potato or rice flour, the rest is wheat flour. Only wheat and rye contain sufficient gluten to make a dough smooth and elastic, enabling it to rise.

WHITE: available in a variety of shapes: French stick, plait, horseshoe roll, high top or loaf. Despite different shape and texture, the nutritional value is essentially the same.

WHOLEMEAL/WHOLEGRAIN/WHOLEWHEAT: made from either 100 percent wholemeal flour or 90 percent wholemeal and 10 percent white flour.

BUTTER
* Good source of energy.
* High in fat.

Butter Storage

Butter not kept in a refrigerator will become soft and melt. As temperatures rise, the fats in butter are oxidised and the oxidisation causes the rancid flavour. Butter should be stored at a low temperature in its original wrapper or a sealed container. Butter can be frozen and will keep for up to 6 months if wrapped in a vapour proof wrap.

CHEESE

Blue Vein
* Good source of protein.
* Excellent source of energy.
* Good source of calcium.
* Good source of sodium.
* High in fat.

Brie
* Useful source of protein.
* Useful source of calcium.
* Useful source of energy.

Camembert
* Useful source of protein.
* Useful source of carotene (which the body converts to Vitamin A).

Cheddar
* Good source of protein.
* Excellent source of calcium.
* Good source of energy.
* Good source of phosphorus.
* Good source of zinc.
* High in fat.

Cottage
* Low in fat.
* Useful source of protein.
* Low cholesterol.

Cream
* Good source of energy.
* High in fat.
* Good source of Vitamin A.

Edam
* Good source of energy.
* Good source of calcium.
* Good source of sodium.
* Good source of magnesium.
* Good source of zinc.

Feta
* Good source of energy.
* Useful source of protein.
* Useful source of Vitamin B1.

Gouda
* Good source of protein.
* Good source of energy.
* Good source of calcium.

Mozzarella
* Good source of protein.
* Good source of energy.
* Excellent source of calcium.

Parmesan
* Excellent source of calcium.
* Good source of energy.
* Excellent source of protein.
* Good source of phosphorus.

Ricotta
* Low in fat.
* Low cholesterol.

Swiss
* Good source of protein.
* Good source of energy.
* Good source of calcium.
* Low in added salt.

Cheese Storage

- Hard cheeses keep for several months.

- Cheddars keep for several weeks.

- Blue vein and stretched curd (mozzarella, haloumy, bocconcini) keep for 1-4 weeks.

- Fresh cheeses (cottage, cream, ricotta) should be used within a week of purchase or by the "use by" date.

- Store cheese in its original wrapper to prevent from drying out. Cover with foil, plastic wrap or place in a plastic container. Plastic wrap is best for surface ripened cheese (brie, camembert, double cream).

- Fresh/soft cheeses absorb flavours and odours. Store them away from other strong foods (including blue vein cheeses).

- Mould can develop on a cheese stored for a long time. Cut it off, re-cover with new

wrap. Use remainder as soon as possible.

☞ Discard soft, unripened cheeses which develop mould (cottage, quark, neufchatel).

☞ Always store cheese in a refrigerator. Never leave it standing in a warm area. Processed cheddar may be stored unrefrigerated until its packaging is opened.

☞ Although not recommended, cheese can be frozen, preferably in its unopened original packet. Small portions of up to 250g thawed slowly in the refrigerator give the best results. Soft cheeses freeze well.

Australian Dairy Corporation

MILK

Milk
* Good source of calcium.
* Good source of protein.
* Good source of lactose.
* Significant source of the B-Group Vitamins.

Hilo/Life
* Excellent source of calcium.
* Good source of protein.
* Reduced fat.
* Good source of lactose.
* Significant source of the B-Group Vitamins.

Lite White
* Excellent source of calcium.
* Good source of protein.
* Low in fat.
* Good source of lactose.
* Significant source of the B-Group Vitamins.

Shape
* Excellent source of calcium.
* Good source of protein.
* Very low in fat.
* Low cholesterol.
* Good source of lactose.
* Significant source of the B-Group Vitamins.

Skim
* Good source of calcium.
* Good source of protein.
* Very low in fat.
* Low cholesterol.
* Low in kilojoules.
* Significant source of the B-Group Vitamins.

NOTE: lactose or milk sugar is a compound of two simple sugars found only in milk. It provides energy in the same way as cane sugar. It stimulates the absorption of calcium, phosphorus and other minerals.

Milk Storage

☞ All dairy foods stored incorrectly will deteriorate.

☞ If stored at a constant 4.5 degrees Celsius (normal household refrigerator temperature), pasteurised milk will keep 10 days; for 2½ days at 10 degrees Celsius, and for 1 day at 15 degrees Celsius.

☞ Keep milk cool, dark and covered.

☞ Milk can be frozen for 4-6 weeks before flavour changes occur. Frozen milk thaws unevenly.

☞ Powdered milk can absorb flavours and moisture and the fat can become rancid. Keep it in a completely dry, sealed container. Store reconstituted milk as other liquid milk.

☞ Keep evaporated and sweetened condensed milk in the refrigerator after opening.

☞ Yoghurt and buttermilk has a storage life of 7-10 days. Store as liquid milk. Freezing is not recommended as it breaks the curd and alters the texture.

☞ Cream behaves in storage much like milk. Natural and soured cream lasts about 7-10 days in the refrigerator. Canned reduced cream will keep for months if unopened. Cream is better suited to freezing than milk, with high fat creams freezing better than lower fat ones. The fat and liquid of cream may separate on thawing, however a light whipping will restore the smoothness.

☞ UHT or Longlife milk may be stored without refrigeration for 6 months after which time, chemical changes may alter flavour. In hot climates these changes will be speeded up so storage life may be shorter.

Apricot
* Good source of copper.
* Good source of iron.
* Rich in carotene (which the body converts to Vitamin A).

Currant
* Good source of iron.
* Good source of protein.
* Good source of calcium.
* Good source of carotene (which the body converts to Vitamin A).
* Natural sugar source gives a quick energy boost.
* Good source of the B-Group Vitamins.

Peach
* Good source of mineral salts potassium, phosphorus and copper).
* Good source of calcium.
* Good source of iron.

Pear
* Good source of Vitamins B1 and B2.
* Good source of calcium.
* Good source of phosphorus.

Prune
* Rich in potassium.
* Good source of fibre.
* Good source of carotene (which the body converts to Vitamin A).
* Excellent source of iron.
* Good source of the B-Group Vitamins.

Raisin
* Excellent source of carbohydrate.
* Good source of energy.
* Low in cholesterol.
* Low in sodium.
* Good source of iron.
* Good source of calcium.
* Good source of the B-Group Vitamins.

Sultana
* Good source of energy (large quantities of sugar, glucose and fructose).
* Good source of fibre.
* Good source of potassium.

Dried Fruit Storage

✏ Store dried fruits in air-tight containers in cupboards; they do not need to be refrigerated.

✏ Prunes should be stored in an air-tight container in the refrigerator as they contain more moisture than other dried fruits.

EGGS
* Good source of iron (each egg yolk provides 1.2mg).
* Valuable source of Vitamin B12.
* Good source of all B-Group Vitamins.
* Vitamins A, D and E are found in the egg yolk, not in the white.
* Good source of minerals (potassium, phosphorous, iodine and zinc).
* All cholesterol is in the yolk.

Egg Storage
Eggs begin to lose quality as soon as they are laid, and it is important to store them correctly. The manner in which eggs are stored can affect their quality more than how long they are stored.

✏ Eggs are best stored in the refrigerator iin their carton, pointed end down – this keeps the yolk centred and prevents damage to the air cell. The carton slows down moisture loss and helps prevent eggs from absorbing other odours in th refrigerator..

Freshness Test
The best guide to freshness is the "use by" date on the carton, but eggs that have been stored correctly can still be edible past this date. Try one of these simple tests.

WATER TEST: place an egg in a bowl of water. Generally a fresh egg will lie at the bottom of the bowl. As the egg ages, the increase in aircell size causes it to float (broad-side up).

BREAK OUT TEST: break the egg onto a flat plate. A fresh egg will have a well-rounded yolk surrounded by a thick gelatinous white that "sits up". As the egg ages the white becomes less gelatinous and the yolk flatter.

✏ It is recommended that eggs NOT be stored in individual egg compartments in the door of the refrigerator.

✏ Egg yolks can be stored for 3 days in the refrigerator. Cover unbroken yolks with a little water. If yolks are broken, press plastic wrap onto the surface to exclude air.

✏ Eggwhites can be stored in an airtight

container in the refrigerator for about 7 days.

☛ Eggs in the shell should not be frozen. However, beaten eggs will freeze successfully. Egg whites also freeze well.

☛ To freeze yolks it is necessary to add 1 teaspoon of salt to six yolks, or 1 tablespoon of sugar to six yolks.

NOTE: the colour of the eggshell bears no relationship to the nutritional value of the egg.

FRUIT AND VEGETABLES

CHECKING FOR FRESHNESS
Avoid buying fruit and vegetables sealed in plastic bags; they become bruised and deteriorate without air.

Vegetables

ARTICHOKES: should have a good bloom on their leaves. Put stems in water when you get them home. Check table overpage.

AVOCADOES: should be firm but give slightly when squeezed gently. Blackened avocadoes are okay for dips.

EGGPLANTS: should be shiny, firm and deeply coloured.

MUSHROOMS: should be firm and dry. Do not buy slimy fungi. Do not buy fungi in sealed plastic bags.

POTATOES: should be firm without any green patches.

TOMATOES: should be firm and red with no wrinkles or spots. Often, organically grown tomatoes have blemishes.

SALAD VEGETABLES: should be bright green with no rotting leaves or brown edges.

Fruit

BANANAS: ripe ones are bright yellow with small brown specks. Under-ripe ones are green.

BERRIES: should be firm, plump, brightly coloured and without wrinkles or broken skin. Eat as soon as possible after buying as they deteriorate quickly.

FIGS: should be plump but soft.

GRAPES: should be shiny, firm and brightly coloured.

MANGOES: should have a fragrant smell and the skin should be orange/yellow coloured.

MELONS: should be plump and firm without soft spots. They should have a sweet smell.

PINEAPPLES: should be firm and fragrant with no damage to the skin. A centre leaf can be pulled out easily if a pineapple is ripe.

Fruit/Vegetable	How to Store	Nutritional Value
APPLES	Refrigerate in vented plastic bags.	*Good source of dietary fibre including pectin.
APRICOTS	Unwrapped in crisper of refrigerator.	*Good source of dietary fibre. *Useful amounts of potassium.
ARTICHOKES (globe)	Refrigerate in vented plastic bags.	*Excellent source of Vitamin C and dietary fibre. *Useful amounts of potassium.
ASPARAGUS	Wrap stem ends in damp absorbent paper; refrigerate.	*Excellent source of Vitamin C. *Good source of dietary fibre. *Useful amounts of Vitamins B1, B2, potassium and iron.
AVOCADOES	Unwrapped in refrigerator.	*Good source of Vitamins E, B6 and folate. *Useful amounts of Vitamin C and potassium. *Some Vitamins B2 and B3. *Avocadoes contain fat in the form of mono-unsaturated fatty acids which can help lower blood cholesterol levels. *Avocadoes do not contain cholesterol.
BANANAS	Unwrapped, at room temperature in a cool, airy place.	*Good source of dietary fibre, Vitamins C and B6. *Useful source of potassium. *Small amounts of other B-Group Vitamins. *Provide complex carbohydrate (sugar bananas give double the amount of regular varieties).
BEANS (French)	Refrigerate in vented plastic bags.	*Very good source of Vitamin C. *Useful amounts of folate and dietary fibre.
BEETROOT	Refrigerate unwrapped after tops have been cut off.	*Good source of folate and dietary fibre. *Useful amounts of Vitamin C. *Small amounts of potassium and iron.
BLUEBERRIES	Cover, refrigerate.	*Good source of Vitamin C.
BROCCOLI	Refrigerate in plastic bags.	*Excellent source of Vitamin C; an average serve provides more than three times the daily need. *Very good source of folate. *Good source of Vitamins B2, B5 and dietary fibre. *Useful amounts of Vitamins E, B6, potassium and iron.
BRUSSELS SPROUTS	Unwrapped in crisper of refrigerator.	*Excellent source of Vitamin C; an average serve provides more than three times the daily need. *Very good source of folate and dietary fibre. *Useful source of Vitamins B2, B6, E, potassium.
CABBAGES	Trim, cover in plastic wrap, refrigerate.	*Excellent source of Vitamin C. *Good source of folate. *Useful source of dietary fibre, potassium and Vitamin B6.
CARROTS	Uncovered in crisper of refrigerator.	*Exceptionally rich in Vitamin A; a large carrot provides about twice the daily need. *Good source of dietary fibre. *Useful source of Vitamin C. *Some Vitamin B6.
CAULIFLOWER	Cut off outer leaves, store in plastic bags in refrigerator.	*Excellent source of Vitamin C: an average serve provides more than twice the daily need. *Good source of dietary fibre. *Useful source of Vitamins B5, B6, folate

Fruit/Vegetable	How to Store	Nutritional Value
		and potassium. *Some Vitamin K.
CELERY	Refrigerate in plastic bag.	*Useful source of Vitamin C and potassium.
CHERRIES	Refrigerate in vented plastic bags.	*Excellent source of Vitamin C. *Useful source of potassium and dietary fibre.
CHOKOES	Uncovered in crisper of refrigerator.	*Good source of Vitamin C.
CORN	Store in husks in plastic bags in refrigerator.	*Excellent source of dietary fibre. *Good source of Vitamins B1 and C, folate, potassium, iron and complex carbohydrate. *Useful source of Vitamins A, B2, B5, B6 and E.
CUCUMBERS	Uncovered in crisper of refrigerator.	*Good source of Vitamin C.
CUMQUATS	Uncovered in crisper of refrigerator.	*Excellent source of Vitamin C. *Good source of dietary fibre.
EGGPLANT	Uncovered in crisper of refrigerator.	*Very good source of Vitamin C. *Useful source of iron. *Some Vitamins A, B2 and dietary fibre.
FENNEL	Uncovered in crisper of refrigerator.	*Good source of Vitamin C. *Some potassium and dietary fibre.
FIGS	Uncovered in crisper of refrigerator.	*Very good source of dietary fibre. *Some potassium.

GRAPEFRUIT	Uncovered in crisper of refrigerator.	*Excellent source of Vitamins B5 and C,
		  half a medium grapefruit provides more than
		  the daily need.
		*Good source of dietary fibre.

GRAPES	Refrigerate in vented plastic bags.	*Good source of Vitamin C and dietary fibre. *Some Vitamin B6 and potassium.
KIWI FRUIT	Uncovered in crisper of refrigerator.	*Excellent source of Vitamin C; one medium kiwi fruit provides twice the daily need. *Some potassium and dietary fibre.
LEEKS	Refrigerate in plastic bags.	*Excellent source of Vitamin C. *Very good source of dietary fibre. *Good source of Vitamins A, B6, E and potassium. *Useful source of Vitamins B1, B2, iron and magnesium.
LEMONS	Refrigerate uncovered.	*Excellent source of Vitamin C. *Some dietary fibre.
LIMES	Uncovered in crisper of refrigerator.	*Excellent source of Vitamin C. *Some dietary fibre.
MANDARINS	Refrigerate uncovered.	*Excellent source of Vitamin C. *Some dietary fibre.
MANGOES	Wrapped in refrigerator.	*Excellent source of Vitamins A and C. *Good source of dietary fibre. *Useful source of Vitamins B1, B6 and potassium.
MELONS	Refrigerate uncovered.	*Excellent source of Vitamin C. *Good source of folate. *Some potassium and dietary fibre. *Rockmelon is a useful source of Vitamin A.

Fruit/Vegetable	How to Store	Nutritional Value
MUSHROOMS	Refrigerate in paper or calico bags or wrapped in absorbent paper.	*Good source of Vitamins B2, B3, B5. *Useful source of Vitamin B12, folate, potassium and dietary fibre.
NECTARINES	Refrigerate uncovered.	*Good source of Vitamin C. *Some Vitamin B3, potassium and dietary fibre.
ORANGES	Refrigerate uncovered.	*Excellent source of Vitamin C; one medium orange will provide more than twice the daily need. *Good source of folate and dietary fibre. *Some Vitamin B1 and potassium.
PASSIONFRUIT	Refrigerate in plastic bags.	*Excellent source of dietary fibre. *Good source of Vitamin C. *Some Vitamin B3.
PEACHES	Refrigerate uncovered.	*Good source of Vitamin C. *Some Vitamin B3, potassium and dietary fibre.
PEARS	Refrigerate uncovered.	*Very good source of dietary fibre.
PEPPERS (capsicum)	Uncovered in crisper of refrigerator.	*One of the richest sources of Vitamin C; one green pepper provides about four times the daily need, and a red peppper twice as much as the green pepper. *Very good source of Vitamin A. *Good source of dietary fibre. *Some potassium.
PINEAPPLES	Refrigerate uncovered.	*Very good source of Vitamin C.
PLUMS	Refrigerate uncovered.	*Useful source of dietary fibre.
PUMPKINS	Uncovered in crisper of refrigerator.	*Excellent source of Vitamins A and C. *Useful source of potassium and dietary fibre. *Some Vitamin E and iron.
RASPBERRIES	Cover, refrigerate.	*One of the best sources of dietary fibre. *Excellent source of Vitamin C. *Useful amounts of iron, potassium and magnesium.
RHUBARB	Refrigerate uncovered.	*Good source of Vitamin C and fibre. *Useful source of Vitamin B1. *Some Vitamin B3.
SNOW PEAS	Refrigerate in plastic bags.	*Excellent source of Vitamin C. *Good source of potassium and dietary fibre. *Useful amounts of Vitamins B5, B6, iron and magnesium.
SPINACH (English)	Uncovered in crisper of refrigerator.	*Excellent source of Vitamin C and folate. *Very good source of Vitamin A. *Good source of Vitamins B2, E and potassium.
STRAWBERRIES	Cover, refrigerate in crisper.	*Excellent source of Vitamin C. *Some folate and dietary fibre.
TOMATOES	Uncovered in crisper of refrigerator.	*Excellent source of Vitamin C. *Good source of Vitamin E, folate and dietary fibre. *Some Vitamin A and potassium.
ZUCCHINIS	Refrigerate in plastic.	*Excellent source of Vitamin C.

MEAT

Beef (lean, grilled)
* Good source of protein.
* Excellent source of iron.
* Good source of Vitamin B3.
* Useful source of Vitamin B2.
* Low in fat.

Chicken (lean, cooked)
* Some iron.
* Good source of Vitamins B3, B1 and B2).
* Some zinc.
* Good source of protein.

Kidneys
* Excellent source of iron.
* Good source of B-Group Vitamins.

Lamb (lean, cooked)
* Good source of iron.
* Good source of zinc.
* Good source of Vitamin B3.
* Useful source of Vitamin B2.
* Valuable protein source.

Liver
* Good source of Vitamin A.
* Good source of iron.
* Good source of B-Group Vitamins and folic acid.

Pork (lean, cooked)
* Good source of iron.
* Good source of zinc.
* Good source of protein.
* Good source of all the B-Group Vitamins.

Veal (lean, cooked)
* Reasonable source of iron.
* Useful source of zinc.
* Useful source of Vitamins B2 and B3.
* Excellent source of protein.

BEEF AND LAMB STORAGE
Fresh meat should always be kept as dry as possible and should not sit in its own "drip". Cold air must circulate freely around it (temperature range of 0 degrees to 4 degrees Celsius). Moisture loss from meat should be kept to a minimum. The more cutting and preparation meat has been subject to, the shorter the storage time. Storage time for mince is less than for steak or chops.

Storage in Meat Compartment
Unwrap meat, arrange in stacks no more than 2-3 layers high, with air space between. Cover top of meat loosely with foil or waxed paper to prevent surface from drying out.

Storage in General Refrigerator
Store in coldest part of refrigerator (at the top in a refrigerator/freezer unit). If meat is to be used within 2 days it can be left in its original packing – either in the meat compartment or in the coldest part of the refrigerator.

Freezing Meat
☞ When freezing meat it is important that air be expelled from the packages, particularly if the meat is cured (such as corned beef). Oxygen left in the package accelerates the oxidisation of fat, giving the meat an "off" flavour after prolonged storage. A vacuum freezer pump will help you extract the air from packages.

☞ If freezing meat, pack in high density polythene bags. Interleave steaks and chops with plastic film if more than one piece is to be placed in a bag. Label, date, exclude all air from bag and seal. Pack meat against coldest surface of the freezer, leaving an air space of 10-15mm between packages and allowing up to 48 hours for meat to freeze.

☞ Meat bought on a styrofoam tray should be repacked properly before freezing. Discard the tray.

☞ NEVER refreeze meat once it has thawed.

☞ Pork juices will coagulate if cooked frozen.

Cooking Meat from the Freezer
CORNED MEATS: allow to defrost in refrigerator before cooking. If cooking straight from frozen state, add 1 tablespoon of salt to cooking liquid.

ROASTS: defrost large joints slowly before cooking. Loosen wrap on joint at base, place on plastic-coated or stainless steel rack in a dish in the main part of the refrigerator. Allow 8 to 10 hours per 500g. DO NOT defrost at room temperature as there is more drip loss and greater risk of bacteria growth. If cooking from the frozen state use a meat thermometer as meat which has been frozen should be cooked to an internal temperature of at least 70 degrees Celsius. At this temperature salmonella (the most common food bacteria) will be killed.

SAUSAGES: defrost in refrigerator as for Roasts.

STEAKS AND CHOPS: cook from frozen state. Brush with oil or butter, grill under HIGH for 3 to 5 minutes each side to seal, reduce heat to MEDIUM and continue cooking until done to taste.

STEWING AND BRAISING MEATS AND MINCE: most recipes are easier to prepare if the meat is defrosted. Follow the method for Roasts.

Microwave Defrosting
Use the Defrost setting, allowing about 5 minutes per serve. If a casserole serves 6, defrosting time should be about 30 minutes. Stir casserole occasionally to distribute heat. Check the manufacturer's instructions with your microwave.

Cooked Meat Dishes Suitable for Freezing
☞ Meat and vegetable soups.

☞ Casseroles, stews and curries.

☞ Minced meat dishes (meatballs, savoury mince, meat sauce).

☞ Sliced roast meats covered with gravy. (Reheat gently as overheating toughens the meat.) Left-over roasts are NOT suitable for freezing unless treated in this way, as moisture and flavour are lost in freezing. The general rule is that the meat dish must have sufficient liquid to cover the meat – add boiled water if necessary. This can be reduced when reheating.

☞ If you intend freezing a particular dish, don't cook it completely as meat is less likely to break up during reheating. Take at least half an hour off the total cooking time when first preparing the dish to be frozen.

☞ Thicken and season casseroles during reheating, rather than before freezing.

To Defrost and Reheat Frozen Meat Dishes
Remove from container and place in oven dish or saucepan. Place in cold oven and set temperature at 150 degrees Celsius. It will take about an hour to defrost. To defrost in a saucepan, set over low heat; this method is much quicker than oven defrosting. Add seasonings as desired while reheating.

Cooking Tips
☞ If using cheaper cuts, use a moist heat method (e.g. casserole or braise) to preserve the meat's natural moisture and tenderness

☞ If using expensive cuts, don't overcook. Too much cooking will toughen these cuts. Large amounts of salt will also toughen meat by drawing out the natural juices.

☞ Marinades tenderise meat – citrus juice, vinegar or wine and herbs will tenderise and impart flavour.

☞ If pounding meat, cover with thick plastic wrap to prevent meat breaking up. Powdered "meat tenderisers" are generally high in salt and should be used sparingly, if at all.

☞ Cutting across the "grain" of meat shortens fibres and ensures tender meat.

Nutrition Tips
☞ Select meat that looks lean.

☞ Trim as much fat off as possible before cooking the meat.

☞ When grilling, allow fat to drain away.

☞ If roasting, use a rack above a dish of water to allow fat to drain away.

☞ If frying, use a non-stick pan to reduce the amount of oil needed.

☞ Allow homemade soups, stews, casseroles and gravies to cool before serving, so that the fat can be easily removed.

MEAT STORAGE GUIDE

MAXIMUM LENGTH OF TIME MEAT SHOULD BE STORED IN REFRIGERATOR:

Corned beef:	**1 week**
Mince and sausages:	**2 days**
Cubed beef and lamb:	**3 days**
Steaks, chops and cutlets:	**4 days**
Roasting joints (with bones in):	**3-5 days**
Roasting joints (boned and rolled):	**2-3 days**
Vacuum packed beef:	**4 weeks**

MAXIMUM LENGTH OF TIME MEAT SHOULD BE FROZEN

BEEF
Joints - solid:	**8 months**
Joints - rolled:	**6 months**
Steaks, stew meat:	**6 months**

LAMB, HOGGET, MUTTON
Joints - bone-in:	**4 months**
Joints - boned and rolled:	**4 months**

VEAL
Joints:	**6 months**
Steaks, chops etc:	**4 months**

MISCELLANEOUS
Corned or cured beef, lamb and tongue:	**1½-2 months in raw state**
	2-4 months in cooked state
Lean minced meats:	**2 months**
Sausages and fatty minced meats:	**1 month**
Offal (fresh)	**1½ -2 months**
Smallgoods:	**1 month**

BASIC CUTS OF BEEF, LAMB AND PORK

BEEF

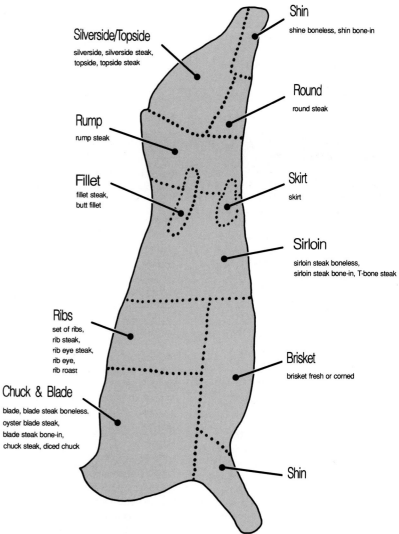

Shin
shine boneless, shin bone-in

Silverside/Topside
silverside, silverside steak, topside, topside steak

Round
round steak

Rump
rump steak

Fillet
fillet steak, butt fillet

Skirt
skirt

Sirloin
sirloin steak boneless, sirloin steak bone-in, T-bone steak

Ribs
set of ribs, rib steak, rib eye steak, rib eye, rib roast

Brisket
brisket fresh or corned

Chuck & Blade
blade, blade steak boneless, oyster blade steak, blade steak bone-in, chuck steak, diced chuck

Shin

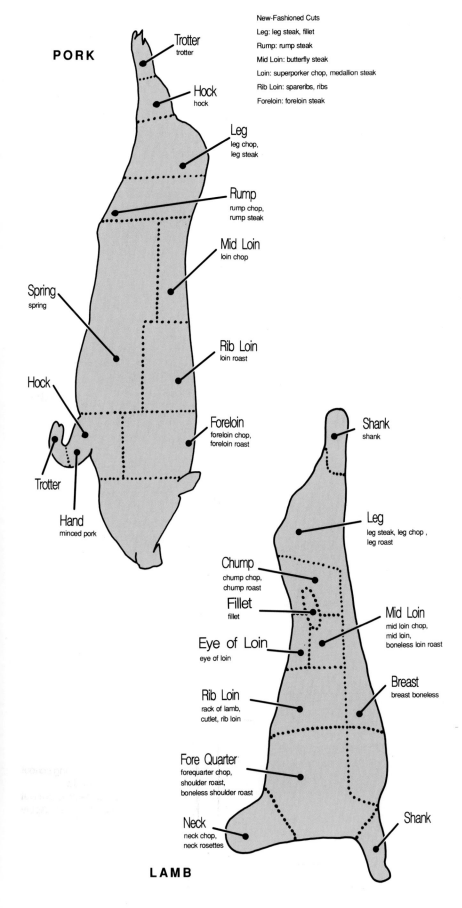

PORK

Trotter
trotter

Hock
hock

New-Fashioned Cuts
Leg: leg steak, fillet
Rump: rump steak
Mid Loin: butterfly steak
Loin: superporker chop, medallion steak
Rib Loin: spareribs, ribs
Foreloin: foreloin steak

Leg
leg chop,
leg steak

Rump
rump chop,
rump steak

Mid Loin
loin chop

Spring
spring

Rib Loin
loin roast

Hock

Foreloin
foreloin chop,
foreloin roast

Trotter

Hand
minced pork

LAMB

Shank
shank

Leg
leg steak, leg chop,
leg roast

Chump
chump chop,
chump roast

Fillet
fillet

Mid Loin
mid loin chop,
mid loin,
boneless loin roast

Eye of Loin
eye of loin

Rib Loin
rack of lamb,
cutlet, rib loin

Breast
breast boneless

Fore Quarter
forequarter chop,
shoulder roast,
boneless shoulder roast

Neck
neck chop,
neck rosettes

Shank

HYGIENE

Pay careful attention to hygiene when han-dling meat as most cases of food poisoning result from leaving food to stand at tempera-tures that permit bacteria to grow.

☞ The longer food spends at temperatures between 5 degrees Celsius and 60 degrees Celsius, the greater the chance of bacteria growing and causing food poisoning.

☞ Food not eaten immediately after cook-ing should be cooled in the refrigerator to below 4 degrees Celsius.

☞ Bacteria can be transferred from one food to another by cooking utensils. Wash all equipment used to handle raw food before using again (eg. chopping boards, tongs, knives, spoons).

☞ Never handle cooked and uncooked meats together. Do not cut them up with the same utensils or on the same boards.

☞ Store cooked meat above raw meat so that blood will not drip down onto the cooked meat.

CARVING MEAT

For easier carving, allow roast meats to "set" in a warm place for 15 to 20 minutes by: turning the oven off and using stored heat, removing the roast and covering with foil, or placing the roast in a preheated warming tray. This ensures moisture is retained.

☞ Remove any string or skewers as you get to them when carving. Always use a carv-ing board. If serving at the table, present the roast on a serving platter, transfer it to carv-ing board for carving, then place sliced meat back on serving tray. This prevents scratches on the platter and damage to the blade.

☞ Use a slicing, not a sawing action, making use of the full length of the blade. Apply only enough pressure to cut meat fibres: too much pressure will bruise or tear the meat.

☞ Carve across the grain where possible to ensure tenderness.

☞ Always serve meat hot. Preheat the plates and serving platter before carving as meat slices lose heat more rapidly than a whole joint.

CARVING EQUIPMENT

KNIVES: have a set of stainless steel knives used solely for carving. Wash knives by hand in hot water straight after use; never put them in the dishwasher. Store knives in a separate drawer to other kitchen utensils.

ELECTRIC CARVING KNIFE: for best results, do not saw or exert pressure, simply guide the blades and bear down across the grain of the meat. After use, turn power off, remove the blades by hand and wash.

FORK: have a carving fork with a guard, two prongs and a long handle.

Crown Roast of Lamb

If a stuffing has been used in the centre of the crown roast, transfer it in serving portions to the serving platter before you begin carving the meat.

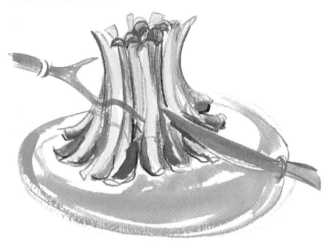

Place crown roast onto carving board. Steady the roast with carving fork, and slice downward between each pair of ribs. Run the knife closely along each rib. Keep close to the bone, always to the right or left, depending on where you started.

Remove chops one at a time by lifting each one onto the knife blade using the fork to steady it). Serve two chops and a portion of stuffing on each plate.

Leg of Lamb

Ask your butcher to remove the pelvic bone.

Place roast on carving board, with shank on carver's right. The inner side of the right leg will be uppermost while the smooth outside portion will be uppermost on a left leg.

Insert carving fork firmly on the left of the leg. Remove two or three slices from the thin side, cutting parallel to the length of the leg.

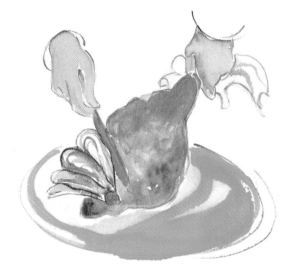

Turn the roast so that it rests on the cut surface; this forms a base. Hold the shank with a clean cloth. Starting at the opposite end, make parallel slices down to the bone.

Rack of Lamb
Place the rack of rib chops on the carving board with the bones facing away from the carver.

You may slice all the way for the full length of the leg bone, then release all the slices by cutting under then, following the top leg of the bone. Alternatively, cut one or two slices then cut across the bottom to release them.

To steady the rack, lightly pierce the meat with the fork at the left end. Make the first cut after the first two bones on the right to make a straight cut.

The rich tasting collar of meat around the shank is the final carving stage. Cut about 8cm below the collar around the bone to release it. Slice the collar into smaller pieces of meat across the grain.

Cut straight down between the second and third rib bones; serve the first two ribs as one chop.

Cut remaining ribs one at a time. Do not cut at an angle or you will have three bones and no meat at the end. To serve, pick up the chop on the flat edge of the knife, holding it firmly with the carving fork.

Boned and Rolled Lamb Joints
The shoulder, forequarter and sometimes the leg are available in the boned and rolled form. Although these cuts may be more expensive per kilogram than their bone-in equivalents, there is no waste when cooking and serving.

A small roast can easily be held with a dessert spoon and fork, placing one on each side of the joint. Slice straight down, or to obtain larger slices, cut diagonally. Slices should be about 2cm thick. No force should be required, as a sharp knife needs little more than guiding through the meat.

Netted Lamb Joints
Netted joints should be raised from the bottom of the baking dish by using a roasting rack. This prevents any possibility of the netting sticking to the dish whilst cooking.

To carve, open the netting at one end of the joint and peel back 5cm. Place the back of the carving fork on the top of the joint to hold it steady, there is no need to pierce the meat. Slice downwards through the joint across the grain. Peel back the netting in stages. This is an easy joint to carve due to the lack of bones, skewers and string.

Rolled Rib Roast

A rolled rib can be carved lying on its side or its end. For a larger roll, lay it on its end with the larger cut surface down and the smaller end up. Sirloin roasts can also be carved using this method.

Lift each slice with the blade of the knife and steady with the fork. Place directly on warmed plate or serving platter. Reinsert the fork progressively lower in the meat each time, keeping the slices uniform. Remove any strings as you come to them. When the roast has only 5-10cm left to carve, divide it down the centre. Lay the cut surface flat on the carving board. Slice as before for both portions.

Insert the carving fork firmly 2-3cm below the top of the roast. Slice across the grain from the right side. Make the first slice thicker than the others so as to get a smooth, level surface from the start.

Bone-In Rib Roast

Carving is easier if you have the backbone removed by the butcher and the rib bones cut short. Usually a rib roast is carved in slices.

Place the rib on a platter with the large end down to form a stable base. Insert the carving fork firmly beneath the top rib. Starting at the right-hand edge (the broadest part), slice the grain horizontally toward the rib side.

Use the tip of the knife to cut along the rib bone to release the slice. Keep close to the bone.

Lift each slice individually by sliding the knife back under the slice and steadying it with the fork. Lift the slice to the side of the platter or to a heated plate.

Fillet of Beef

Hold the fillet in place with the back of a fork. Try not to pierce the meat. Begin slicing at the wide end of the fillet, keeping the blade of the knife slightly tilted and carving across the grain. Make slices about 2cm thick. To keep the warmth and the juices within the slices, stack them closely together on one side of the carving board as they are cut.

Corned Silverside

Place the meat, fat side up, on the carving board, with the tip to the right of the carver. Check the direction of the grain, if you are not sure how it runs cut off a thin slice to be sure.

Begin slicing at the tip, slicing across the grain, to ensure tenderness.

Cut small amount of breast meat away with wing, then bend wing away from body to find joint where wing joins body; cut through this. Repeat for other wing.

Cut through skin connecting legs to body. Using your fingers, find the joints between the legs and body and cut through these. The cuts consisting of the legs and thighs are called marylands.

Cut leg pieces into two to give thigh and drumstick.

Separate breast and back by cutting through rib bones along each side of body – cutting close to backbone.

Cut along breastbone to divide breast into two pieces. Trim excess fat and skin from all pieces.

HOW TO COOK THE MEAT YOU BUY

This basic guide will help you to make the most of the meat you buy; simply match the meat and cooking methods for great results.

	Pan fry	Crumb fry	Grill	Barbecue	Oven roast	Pot roast	Casserole	Steam
BEEF								
Blade steaks	▲	▲	▲	▲	▲	▲	▲	
Brisket						▲	▲	▲
Chuck steaks						▲	▲	
Fillet, rib/rib eye, sirloin, t-bone steaks	▲		▲	▲	▲			
Lean mince	▲	▲	▲	▲	▲		▲	
Roasts – topside, sirloin, rib, blade, chuck					▲			
Round/minute steaks	▲	▲	▲	▲		▲	▲	
Rump steaks	▲		▲	▲	▲			
Spare ribs	▲		▲	▲	▲		▲	
Shin							▲	
Silverside steaks	▲		▲	▲				
Silverside			▲		▲	▲	▲	▲
Skirt (rolled and seasoned)					▲	▲	▲	
Topside steaks		▲		▲	▲	▲	▲	
LAMB								
Breast					▲			
Chump chops, leg chops/steaks, mid loin chops/steaks/noisettes	▲		▲	▲	▲			
Eye of loin, lamb fillet	▲		▲	▲				
Forequarter chops	▲		▲	▲	▲	▲	▲	
Lean mince	▲	▲	▲	▲	▲		▲	
Leg roast					▲			
Neck chops/cutlets Rib loin chops/cutlets (rack of lamb)	▲	▲	▲	▲	▲			
Roasts – shoulder, chump, mid-loin, rib-loin, forequarter					▲			

	Pan fry	Crumb fry	Grill	Barbecue	Oven roast	Pot roast	Casserole	Steam
Shoulder chops	▲		▲	▲				
Spare ribs	▲		▲	▲	▲			

VEAL

	Pan fry	Crumb fry	Grill	Barbecue	Oven roast	Pot roast	Casserole	Steam
Breast					▲			
Eye of loin	▲		▲	▲				
Fillet steaks, rump/rump steaks, spare ribs	▲		▲	▲	▲			
Forequarter chops/steaks, shoulder steaks	▲	▲	▲	▲	▲	▲	▲	
Knuckle, neck							▲	
Leg steaks/schnitzels/chops, loin chops/cutlets	▲	▲	▲	▲	▲			
Shoulder roasts					▲	▲		

NEW-FASHIONED PORK

	Pan fry	Crumb fry	Grill	Barbecue	Oven roast	Pot roast	Casserole	Steam
Butterfly steaks	▲	▲	▲	▲	▲	▲	▲	
Diced pork	▲	▲	▲	▲		▲	▲	
Leg schnitzel	▲	▲				▲	▲	
Leg steaks/shoulder chops	▲	▲	▲	▲		▲	▲	
Loin fillet	▲		▲	▲	▲	▲	▲	▲
Loin chops	▲	▲	▲	▲	▲	▲	▲	
Medallion steaks/loin	▲	▲	▲	▲	▲	▲	▲	
Mince	▲	▲	▲	▲	▲	▲	▲	▲
Roasts – leg, loin, neck, cotch boneless, shoulder, forequarter					▲	▲	▲	
Spareribs	▲		▲	▲	▲	▲	▲	

Compiled with the assistance of the Australian Meat and Livestock Corporation and the Australian Pork Corporation

SEAFOOD

* High in protein.
* Low in kilojoules.
* Low in cholesterol.
* Rich in phosphorus.
* Rich in iron.
* Rich in iodine.
* Good source of omega-3 fatty acids.

NOTE: omega-3's can reduce blood fats, decrease blood pressure and prevent blood clots forming to block arteries. They may also be beneficial in helping with certain types of arthritis and skin conditions.

TYPES OF SEAFOOD

Fish can be divided in two types: fat/oily and lean/dry.

FAT/OILY FISH: mullet, pilchards, mackerel, tuna, tailor. Fat or oil content varies with species and sometimes the season. Oily fish is suitable for baking, grilling and barbecuing. Kilojoule content is similar to lean fish.

LEAN/DRY FISH: flathead, snapper, bream, gemfish, john dory, mirror dory, trevally and ling. Lean fish are preferred for pan-frying, steaming or poaching, but can be grilled or baked if kept moist. Fat content is less than two percent.

CRUSTACEANS: yabbies, lobsters, crabs, prawns, balmain bugs, moreton bay bugs.

MOLLUSCS: cuttlefish, abalone, oysters, mussels, pippies, cockles.

SHELLFISH: scallops, squid, octopus.

WHAT TO LOOK FOR WHEN BUYING SEAFOOD

Fillets and Cutlets

- Flesh should be shiny and firm, not dull and soft.
- Flesh should not be "water-logged".
- Should have a pleasant sea smell.
- No discolouration.

Shellfish

- Lobsters, crabs and balmain bugs should have no discolouration of joints.
- Prawns should have no discolouration along the edges of segments of legs.
- Shells of molluscs, such as scallops and mussels should be tightly closed.
- Should have a pleasant sea smell.

Whole Fish

- Bright red gills.
- Firm flesh, springs back when touched.
- Eyes bright, not sunken. Skin bright and lustrous.
- Should have a pleasant sea smell.

FISH STORAGE

Whole Fish

- Scale, and remove gills and gut.
- Wash in cold water and dry well.
- Wrap in aluminium foil or place the fish in a covered container.
- Store in refrigerator.
- Use within 2-3 days of purchase.

Fillets and cutlets

- Wash in cold water and dry well.
- Wrap in aluminium foil or place in a covered container.
- Store in refrigerator.
- Use within 2-3 days of purchase.

Smoked fish

- Wrap in aluminium foil or place in a covered container.
- Store in refrigerator.
- Use within 7-10 days of purchase.

NOTE: live mussels, oysters, pippies and cockles will die if placed in refrigerator. It is best to keep these in a cool, dark place such as the laundry. During cool weather they will stay alive for approximately 3 days. Discard any that open prior to cooking.

FREEZING SEAFOOD

Fish

Seafood should be absolutely fresh when purchased for the home freezer. Freeze whole fish only if you want to serve it whole, as filleting a frozen or thawed out fish does not produce satisfactory fillets. Gut and gill whole fish before placing in freezer. Wrap each fish/fillet/cutlet individually in plastic wrap, this enables you to thaw out exactly what is required for the family meal. Label, date and freeze. As soon as the fish is frozen, remove and dip in cold water, this forms an ice glaze; return to freezer. The glaze helps protect the frozen food from drying out and developing "off flavours".
FREEZER LIFE: 4-6 months. Mullet can be kept 3 months due to fat content.

Shellfish

Clean and remove inedible portions. Wash and wrap large specimens such as lobsters or crabs separately. With smaller species, such as prawns, it is best to freeze in block form, i.e. place prawns in freezable container, cover with cold water, freeze, label and date. Ice-cream containers are ideal.
FREEZER LIFE: 2-3 months

NOTE: when thawing shellfish it is best done in a refrigerator. However, fish is far better cooked in its frozen state.

Cooking Frozen Seafood

Frozen seafood, especially fish fillets, are easier to batter or crumb – so don't thaw them out completely. Frozen seafood holds its shape well and fish flavour and texture is not lost if fish is cooked in this way.

Thawing a Whole Fish

Place in lower section of refrigerator 24 hours before required, or use a microwave on Defrost setting.

CHOLESTEROL CONSIDERATIONS

High levels of cholesterol in the blood can cause blood vessels to clog. If those vessels supplying the heart block completely, a heart attack results. The amount of cholesterol you produce depends on several factors, but mostly on the type of fat you eat.

The Australian Heart Foundation recommends that all adults find out their cholesterol level. An amount of less than 5.5 millimoles (mmol) per litre of blood is desirable. (A millimole is an international unit of measurement for blood cholesterol.) A simple test by your doctor will reveal your cholesterol level.

Cholesterol has different sources. We produce cholesterol naturally in our bodies; it is also found in all foods of animal origin - meat, milk, butter, cheese, cream and eggs.

SATURATED FATS: can result in raised blood cholesterol levels so eat less of these. Cut down on butter, cream, cheese, milk, egg yolks, offal, cakes, chocolates, biscuits, potato crisps, ice cream and meat pies.

POLYUNSATURATED FATS: are found mostly in vegetable foods and polyunsaturated vegetable oils such as safflower, sunflower, maize, soy bean and grape seed oil and polyunsaturated margarine. Although these can't be eaten without care, they can largely replace saturated fats in our diet. Fish also contains polyunsaturated fats.

MONO-UNSATURATED FATS: are found in avocadoes, olives, peanuts, olive oil and peanut oil. They do not raise your cholesterol level but are high in kilojoules and intake should be limited.

Follow these simple guidelines:

- Eat fewer fatty foods.
- Avoid fatty and processed meats.
- Eat more bread, cereals, fruit and vegetables.
- Cut down on salt.
- Drink less alcohol.
- Exercise daily.
- Eat low-fat milk, yoghurt and cheese.
- Eat lean meat – remove visible fat from steak, chops, and skin and fat from chicken. If your family eats a lot of mince, select a lean cut of meat and ask the butcher to mince it for you.

Fish Marketing Authority

TO CLEAN A FISH

Using a sharp knife, cut down the belly from the vent to the head. Pull out the entrails. Wash fish thoroughly and pat dry with paper towel.

TO SCALE A FISH

Grip the fish firmly by the tail, using the edge of a blunt knife, scrape from the tail to the head. Repeat on other side.

Starting at head, cut flat against spine; move knife towards tail with a "press and gentle push" motion. Turn fish over, repeat on other side).

For a flat fish: Cut through centre of fish along spine from head towards tail. Carefully cut flesh away from fish, scraping blade along bones as you cut.

TO FILLET A FISH

Place fish on chopping board and hold firmly. For a round fish: Using a sharp knife, cut through half of fish along front fin .

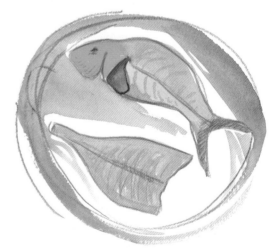

TO SHELL PRAWNS

Hold head of prawn firmly and twist to remove from body of prawn.

Remove shell and legs from body without removing tail shell.

Remove the two tail fins.

Slip tail shell from prawn.

Remove back vein from prawn, pulling gently.

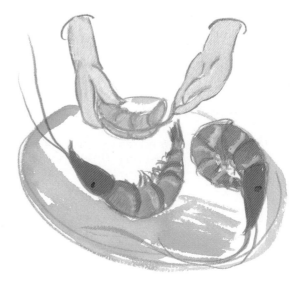

Turn lobster around and cut through head in same way.

Lobsters can be bought alive or cooked. Their flesh is white and firm and has a delicate flavour.

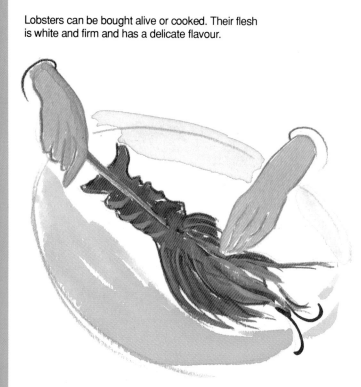

Pull lobster halves apart. Discard white gills and grey thread running down centre back of tail. Remove meat from all sections of lobster using your fingers.

TO PREPARE A COOKED LOBSTER
Place lobster back-down on stable surface, cut through chest and tail with sharp knife.

Vegetarians need to eat a variety of foods to maintain a balanced diet.

Complete proteins are from animal sources (eggs, red meat, chicken, fish, dairy products) and contain the eight elements of protein called amino acids. Protein in a completely vegetarian diet is supplied by grains, legumes, nuts, seeds and some vegetables such as potatoes. They are known as secondary or incomplete proteins because they are either low or completely lacking in one or more essential amino acids.

Vegetable protein when properly combined can give protein equal in value to that from animal sources. Protein combining is evident in the cultures of Mexico (bean and corn), India (rice and lentils), Asia (rice and bean curd)and in Europe (milk and potatoes). Common combinations in Australia are bread and cheese, milk and cereal, even peanut butter and bread; these are known as complementary proteins. The most recognised of these protein groups are: dairy food and grains, dairy food and legumes, dairy food and potatoes, legumes and nuts, grains and legumes.

For a healthy, well-balanced diet include a range of different legumes (lentils, borlotti, haricot, kidney or butter beans, chick peas, peanuts and soy products), numerous wholegrain products (grains, breads, cereals), dairy products (low fat if possible), eggs and lots of fruit and vegetables.

Vitamin B12 is found mainly in food of animal origin and could be lacking in a total vegetarian diet. It is present in milk, cheese, eggs, yoghurt and mushrooms and also occurs in fermented soya bean products such as tofu..

NUTRIENTS

WHAT SUPPLIES THEM
Further details are given under each food section in the chapter.

PROTEIN: beef, dairy products, eggs, fish, game, lamb, milk, nuts, potatoes, poultry, pulses, wholemeal bread, wholemeal pasta.

CARBOHYDRATES: cereal grains, potatoes, vegetables, wholemeal flour.

FATS & OILS: animal fats, butter, cheese, cooking fats and oils, fish oils, margarine, milk, nuts.

VITAMINS & MINERALS: a variety of foods of plant and animal origin, particularly fruit and vegetables.

FIBRE: apples, bananas, bran, brown rice, corn, dried fruit, green vegetables, muesli, nuts, oranges, potatoes in their jackets, pulses, rhubarb, wholemeal bread, wholemeal pasta (white rice and pasta are low in fibre).

VITAMINS AND MINERALS

WHAT THEY DO

VITAMIN A: builds healthy eyes, tissue, skin and mucous membranes.

VITAMIN B-GROUP: promotes digestion, nourishes nervous system. (Includes B1 (thiamin), B2 (riboflavin), B3 (niacin), B6, B12, folic acid). Needed for production of red blood cells, healthy skin and hair and assists brain functioning.

VITAMIN C (ascorbic acid): essential for growth, renews tissues, cares for skin, hair, teeth and gums. Helps fight against infection, maintains healthy muscles, ligaments and tendons. Promotes healing.

VITAMIN D: needed for bone development, especially in the very young and the elderly. Helps the body absorb calcium from the intestine and regulates the amount entering the bone from the blood.

VITAMIN E: helps prevent circulatory problems.

VITAMIN K: essential vitamin for normal blood clotting.

Minerals

CALCIUM: builds bones and healthy teeth. An important mineral for many metabolic processes.

COPPER: helps form red blood cells.

IRON: essential for formation of red blood cells and muscle cells.

MAGNESIUM: as for calcium. Deficiency can cause weakness.

PHOSPHORUS: as for calcium.

POTASSIUM: regulates state of fluids in body cells, in particular the muscle cells and blood cells. Helps bone structure.

PROTEIN: helps build and repair body tissues.

Preserving Vitamins and Minerals
Vitamins can be destroyed during cooking and preparation. Water-soluble vitamins, such as the B-Group Vitamins, are destroyed by light. Vitamins A, D and E are not water-soluble so are not destroyed by cooking.

➤ Vegetable water contains vitamins and minerals. Don't throw it away, use it in soups or sauces. Don't keep spinach water; it contains oxalic acid which prevents absorption of calcium.

➤ Green vegetables will lose more Vitamin C if kept in a warm dish; eat them as soon as they are cooked.

➤ Prepare salads at the last minute because cutting exposes the vitamins to light.

➤ Lemon juice in salads helps preserve Vitamin C (use it in preference to vinegar).

FOOD ADDITIVES

Most of the processed food we buy contain food additives approved by the National Health and Medical Research Council.

Unfortunately some food additives can trigger allergic reactions such as headaches, rashes, breathlessness or even asthma. Many asthmatics are allergic to sulphur (preservative 220)and its derivatives. Check with your doctor if you suspect you suffer from any allergic reaction after eating a specific food. If an allergy is identified, you can avoid particular foods.

Australian food regulations determine and control the amount and type of food additives added to particular foods.

In Australia it is necessary to include on all package labels a list, in descending order by weight, including all the ingredients that have gone into a food. In order to make it easier to list all the different food additives on one label they are now identified using an internationally approved code numbering system.

Food additives are added to foods to: retain their nutritional value and wholesomeness, maintain or improve their keeping qualities and to make food more attractive by enhancing its taste, colour or consistency.

The following is a list of the types of additives and their corresponding numbers. Under each class name there is a brief description of their nature and function.

Colours
These add colour or restore colour losses that have occurred during processing and storage, and ensure a uniform colour in the finished product. Natural and synthetic colours are used to enhance the appearance of foods. Approved synthetic colours are used when there is not enough stable natural colours available.

100	Curcumin, Turmeric
101	Riboflavin
102*	Tartrazine
107*	Yellow 2G
110*	Sunset yellow FCF
120	Cochineal, Carmines
122*	Azorubine, Carmoisine
123*	Amaranth
124*	Poncear 4R, brilliant scarlet
127*	Erythrosine
129*	Allura red AC
132*	Indigotine
133*	Brilliant blue FCF
140	Chlorophyll
142*	Food green S
150	Caramel
151*	Brilliant black BN
153	Carbon black
155*	Brown HT

160	. . . . Carotene
160	ß-apo-8' Carotenoic acid methyl ester
160(a)	. . . . ß-Carotene
160(b)*	. . . . Annatto extracts
160(e)	. . . . . ß-apo-8' Carotenal
160(f)	ß-apo-8' Carotenoic acid ethyl ester
161	. . . . Xanthophylls
161(g)	. . . . Canthaxanthin
162	. . . . Beet red
163	. . . . .Anthocyanins
171	. . . . Titanium dioxide
172	. . . . Iron oxide

* Synthetic Colours

Preservatives

Only a few additives are approved as preservatives. They are used to prolong the shelf-life of foods by controlling the growth of mould, bacteria and yeasts.

200	. . . . Sorbic acid
201	. . . . Sodium sorbate
202	. . . . Potassium sorbate
203	. . . . Calcium sorbate
210	. . . . Benzoic acid
211	. . . . Sodium benzoate
212	. . . . Potassium benzoate
213	. . . . Calcium benzoate
216	. . . . Propylparaben
218	. . . . Methylparaben
220	. . . . .Sulphur dioxide
221	. . . . Sodium sulphite
222	. . . . Sodium bisulphite
223	. . . . . . Sodium metabisulphite
224	. . . . . . Potassium metabisulphite
225	. . . . . . Potassium sulphite
228	. . . . . . Potassium bisulphite
234	. . . . Nisin
280	. . . . Propionic acid
281	. . . . Sodium propionate
282	. . . . .Calcium propionate
283	. . . . . . Potassium propionate

Anti-oxidants

Used to retard the oxidation process in foods. This prevents or limits oxidation and rancidity in foods containing fats and oils, and the browning process in fruit products. Antioxidants help retain food's attractiveness and stabilises the flavour for longer periods.

300	. . . . .Ascorbic acid
301	. . . . Sodium ascorbate
302	. . . . Calcium ascorbate
303	. . . . Potassium ascorbate
304	. . . . Ascorbyl palmitate
306	. . . . Tocopherols
307	. . . . dl-α-Tocopherol
308	. . . . γ-Tocopherols
309	. . . . δ-Tocopherol
310	. . . . Propyl gallate
311	. . . . Octyl gallate
312	. . . . Dodecyl gallate
317	. . . . Erythorbic acid
318	. . . . . . Sodium erythorbate
319	. . . . Tert-Butylhydroquinone
320	.Butylated hydroxyanisole
321	. . . . Butylated hydroxytoluene
322	. . . . Lecithins

Food Acids

Used to maintain a constant acid level in foods despite variations in the acid level of ingredients.

260	. . . . .Acetic acid
261	. . . . Potassium acetate
262	. . . . Sodium acetate
263	. . . . Calcium acetate
264	. . . . Ammonium acetate
270	. . . . Lactic acid
296	. . . . Malic acid
297	. . . . .Fumaric acid
325	. . . . .Sodium lactate
326	. . . . Potassium lactate
327	. . . . Calcium lactate
328	. . . . .Ammonium lactate
329	. . . . .Magnesium lactate
330	. . . . Citric acid
331	. . . . .Sodium acid citrate
331	. . . . Sodium citrate
331	. . . Sodium dihydrogen citrate
332	. . . . Potassium citrate
333	. . . . .Calcium citrate
334	. . . . Tartaric acid
335	. . . . Sodium tartrate
336	. . . . .Potassium acid tartrate
336	. . . . Potassium tartrate
337	. . . . Potassium sodium tartrate
338	. . . . Phosphoric acid
350	. . . . DL-Sodium malate
350	. . . . .DL-Sodium hydrogen malate
351	. . . . Potassium malate
352	. . . . . . DL-Calcium malate
353	. . . . Metatartaric acid
354	. . . . Calcium tartrate
355	. . . . Adipic acid
357	. . . . Potassium adipate
365	. . . . Sodium fumarate
366	. . . . Potassium fumarate
367	. . . . Calcium fumarate
380	. . . . Triammonium citrate
381	. . . . . Ferric ammonium citrate

Vegetable Gums

Ensure food consistency. Vegetable gums come from vegetable sources and are used to modify the texture of foods.

400	. . . . Alginic acid
401	. . . . Sodium alginate
402	. . . . Potassium alginate
403	. . . . Ammonium alginate
404	. . . . Calcium algenate
405	. . . . . Propylene glycol alginate
406	. . . . .Agar
407	. . . . Carrageenan
410	. . . . Locust bean gum
412	. . . . Guar gum
413	. . . . Tragacanth
414	. . . . .Acacia
415	. . . . Xanthan gum
416	. . . . Karaya gum
440(a)	. . . . Pectin
461	. . . . Methylcellulose
464	. . .Hydroxypropylmethyl cellulose
466	. . . Sodium carboxymethyl cellulose
1450	. . . Starch sodium octenylsuccinate

Humectants

Prevent foods from drying out. Only three additives are used here as humectants.

420	. . . . Sorbitol
421	. . . . Mannitol
422	. . . . Glycerin
965	. . . Hydrogenated glucose syrups
967	. . . . Xylitol
1200	. . . . Polydextrose
1518	. . . . Triacetin
1520	. . . . .Propylene glycol

Emulsifiers

Prevent oil and water mixtures from separating into layers in the final product, maintaining a uniform mix.

433	. . . . Polysorbate 80
435	. . . . Polysorbate 60
436	. . . . Polysorbate 65
442	Ammonium salts of phosphatidic acids
471	. . . . . . .Glyceryl monostearate
471	. . . . .Mono and diglycerides
	of fat forming fatty acids
472(a)	. . . . Acetic and fatty acid esters
	of glycerol
472(b)	. . . . .Lactic and fatty acid esters
	of glycerol
472(c)	. . . . . Citric and fatty acid esters
	of glycerol
472(d)	. . . . Tartaric and fatty acid esters
	of glycerol
472(e)	. . . Diacetyltartaric and fatty acid

esters of glycerol

473 . . . . . Sucrose esters of fatty acids

476 . Polyglycerol esters of interesterified ricinoleic acid

491 . . . . Sorbitan monostearate

Thickeners

Ensure food consistency. Thickeners include such things as starches and are used to thicken foods.

441 . . . . Gelatine
1400 . . . . Dextrins
1403 . . . . Bleached starches
1404 . . . . Oxidised starches
1405 . . . . . Enzyme treated starches
1410 . . . . . . Monostarch phosphate
1412 . . . . Distarch phosphate
1413 . . . Phosphated starch phosphate
1414 . . . Acetylated distarch phosphate
1420 . . . . Starch acetate, esterified with acetic anhydride
1421 . . . . . . Starch acetate esterified, with vinyl acetate
1422 . . . . . Acetylated distarch adipate
1440 . . . . Hydroxypropyl starch
1442 . Hydroxypropyl distarch phosphate
1450 . . Starch sodium octenylsuccinate

Flavour Enhancers

Bring out the flavour of foods without giving a flavour of their own.

620 . . . . L-glutamic acid
621 . . . . Monsodium L-glutamate
622 . . . . . . Monopotassium L-glutamate
623 . . . . . . Calcium di-L-glutamate
625 . . . . . . Magnesium di-L-glutamate
624 . . . . Monoammonium L-glutamate
627 . . . . Disodium guanylate
631 . . . . Disodium inosinate

Mineral Salts

Enhance the texture of foods such as processed meats which might lose fat and meat juices. Includes such things as carbonates and phosphates which are used to improve the physical stability of foods.

170 . . . . Calcium carbonate
339 . . . . Sodium phosphate
340 . . . . Potassium phosphate
343 . . . . Magnesium phosphate
450 . . . . Potassium metaphosphate
450 . . . . . . Potassium pyrophosphate
450 . . . . . . Sodium metaphosphate
450 . . . . Sodium pyrophosphate
450 . . . . . . Sodium polyphosphates
450(a) . . . . . . Ammonium phosphate
500 . . . . Sodium bicarbonate

500 . . . . Sodium carbonate
501 . . . . .Potassium bicarbonate
501 . . . . Potassium carbonate
503 . . . . Ammonium bicarbonate
503 . . . . Ammonium carbonate
504 . . . . Magnesium carbonate
509 . . . . Calcium chloride
511 . . . . Magnesium chloride
529 . . . . Calcium oxide

Flour Treatment Agents

Improve flour performance in bread making.

223 . . . . .Sodium metabisulphite
300 . . . . Ascorbic acid
341 . . . . Calcium phosphate
481 . . . . . . .Sodium stearoyl lactylate
482 . . . . . . Calcium stearoyl lactylate
510 . . . . Ammonium chloride
516 . . . . Calcium sulphate
920 . . . .L-Cysteine monohydrochloride
924 . . . . Potassium bromate

Anti-caking Agents

Ensure that products such as salt flow freely when poured.

460 . . . . . . Cellulose microcrystalline
460 . . . . Cellulose powdered
504 . . . . Magnesium carbonate
536 . . . . . . Potassium ferrocyanide
542 . . . . Bone phosphate
551 . . . . Silicon dioxide
552 . . . . Calcium silicate
554 . . . . . Sodium aluminosilicate
556 . . . . .Calcium aluminium silicate
570 . . . . Stearic acid
572 . . . . Magnesium stearate

Propellants

Used in aerosol containers.

290 . . . . Carbon dioxide
931 . . . . .Nitrogen
932 . . . . .Nitrous oxide

Bleaching Agents

Whiten foods such as flour.

925 . . . . Chlorine
926 . . . . Chlorine dioxide
928 . . . . Benzoyl peroxide

Other Food Additives

Includes free-flowing agents, anti-foaming agents, flavour enhancers, curing agents, bleaching and maturing agents.

181 . . . . Tannic acid
235 . . . . Natamycin
249 . . . . Potassium nitrite
250 . . . . Sodium nitrite
251 . . . . Sodium nitrate

262 . . . . Sodium diacetate
465 . . . . Methyl ethyl cellulose
469 . . . . Sodium caseinate
475 . . . Polyglycerol esters of fatty acids
480 . . . Dioctyl sodium sulphosuccinate
492 . . . . Sorbitan tristearate
508 . . . . Potassium chloride
514 . . . . Sodium sulphate
515 . . . . Potassium sulphate
518 . . . . Magnesium sulphate
519 . . . . Cupric sulphate
526 . . . . .Calcium hydroxide
541 . . . . Sodium aluminium phosphate
553(b) . . . . Talc
558 . . . . Bentonite
559 . . . . Kaolin
575 . . . . Glucono δ-lactone
577 . . . . Potassium gluconate
578 . . . . .Calcium gluconate
579 . . . . Ferrous gluconate
636 . . . . Maltol
637 . . . . Ethyl maltol
900 . . . . Dimethylpolysiloxane
901 . . . . Beeswax, white
901 . . . . .Beeswax, yellow
903 . . . . .Carnauba wax
904 . . . . Shellac, bleached
905 . . . . . . .Mineral oil, white
905 . . . . Petrolatum
1201 . . . . Polyvinylpyrrolidone
1202 . . . . . . Polyvinylpolyprrolidone
1505 . . . . Triethyl citrate
1510 . . . . .Ethyl alcohol
1517 . . . . Glycerol diacetate

Miscellaneous Additives & Processing Aids

ARTIFICIAL SWEETENERS: used to sweeten low-joule foods instead of sugar.

ENZYMES: break down foods such as milk into curds and whey.

FLAVOURS: restore losses during processing and maintain uniformity. They are added to foods to give a wide variety of flavoursome products without restriction of season or geographical location.

MINERALS: added to certain foods to supplement dietary intake

VITAMINS: make up for losses in processing and storage and are added to certain foods to supplement dietary intake.

Information contained in this chapter was compiled with the assistance of the Australian Dairy Corporation, the Bread Research Institute of Australia, the Fish Marketing Authority, Milk Marketing NSW, NSW Egg Corporation, NSW Meat Marketing Authority, the National Health and Medical Research Council and the Nutrition Education Service.

CLEANING

Prior to 1907, the use of synthetic detergents to remove dirt and grime was unheard of. Soap and water were the common cleaning agents before fluorescers, deodorisers, disinfectants and solvents became so much a part of our way of life. Cleaning agents should be effective and safe but many products continue to be sold which are not readily biodegradable. Biodegradable means 'capable of being decomposed by living organisms such as bacteria'; try to use these cleaners in preference to others. "Green" cleaners are listed on page 62.

✐ Establish a cleaning routine. Some parts of the house need cleaning more often than others: the bathroom and the kitchen need daily attention. Wipe down the toilet and hand basin each day; clean the kitchen sink daily and mop the floors as often as possible. Divide your cleaning into daily, weekly, monthly, even yearly chores. Don't try to do everything at once!

✐ Read all labelling carefully.

✐ Use less of everything – two squirts of washing-up liquid does not clean twice as well! Allow plates and pans to soak in order to minimise use of detergents and water.

CARPETS

Vacuum the main living areas daily, if possible, and at least weekly. Don't wait until the carpet looks dirty.

☞ Before you vacuum, pick up all toys, buttons, pins, coins, leaves and as many threads as possible.

☞ To keep carpet in good condition, shampoo about once a year. Shampoo before a carpet gets too dirty; dirt left for long periods can be impossible to remove.

☞ A dry foam carpet shampoo crystallises and absorbs the dirt particles; colours will be less likely to run. Other detergents may contain bleaches which can damage carpets.

☞ Small cotton rugs can be machine washed.

☞ Don't wet carpets too much as they will be difficult to dry and more likely to run. If the carpet backing gets too wet, fungus may occur.

☞ A mechanical shampooer does a thorough job. Before you start, vacuum the carpet well (about 10-12 strokes over each section). Check colours won't run by testing shampoo on a hidden piece of carpet. Dilute shampoo, follow manufacturers instructions. Vacuum when carpet is dry to remove any leftover foam and raise the carpet pile, replace furniture.

☞ Don't walk on wet carpet as it may cause damage.

CLEANING AND DEODORISING A CARPET: mix 2 parts cornflour with 1 part borax. Sprinkle liberally on carpet, leave 1 hour, then vacuum.

FOR TOUGHER STAINS: repeatedly blot with vinegar in soapy water. Quick deodorising can be done by sprinkling bicarbonate of soda on the carpet, then vacuuming.

CURTAINS

☞ Remove dust and dirt with a vacuum cleaner (not brush attachment).

☞ Always test colours before washing curtains. Remove hooks and weights.

☞ Small curtains can be washed, but large curtains should be professionally cleaned.

☞ NEVER soak rayon or silk curtains.

☞ NEVER iron plastic curtains.

☞ NEVER machine wash, twist or iron fibreglass curtains or dry clean them.

☞ Wash delicate fabrics by hand.

☞ Soak net curtains in warm sudsy water in a large container so they can be moved around. DO NOT rub or twist. Dip freshly washed curtains in starch to add crispness.

CUSHIONS

☞ Cover cushions with removable covers which can easily be washed.

☞ Do not overwet cushion fillings as this can cause fillings to lump together or to rot.

FLOORS

CONCRETE: clean with damp mop. Don't use soap as it's difficult to rinse off.

CORK: if sealed, mop occasionally. If polished, coat with wax polish a few times a year. Never let cork get too wet, it may crack. Vinyl-coated tiles should be mopped sparingly with a detergent solution when dirty. Alternatively, substitute half a cup of vinegar for detergent in a bucket of water .

LINOLEUM: wash floor with warm, soapy water.

MARBLE: don't use abrasive cleansers, seek professional advice if floor becomes stained. Wipe over with a damp soft mop dipped in diluted biodegradable washing-up detergent. Oil, fats and acids can damage marble. Don't get floor too wet.

PAINTED: glossy enamel paint can be washed with hot water. Rub gently. Mop with a mild detergent using a little water.

QUARRY TILE: clean with damp mop and warm soapy water. Treat a newly laid floor with linseed oil and don't wash it for two weeks. White patches can be wiped with a weak solution of vinegar and water.

SLATE/STONE: wash with washing soda dissolved in water. Do not wash with soap, it will leave a film.

WOODEN: sanded and sealed floors need to be damp mopped. Don't use very hot water and never soak the floor. Polished wood shouldn't need washing. Sweep regularly, polish occasionally.

FURNISHING FABRICS

☞ Fitted covers can be cleaned using a dry foam upholstery shampoo. The basic rules are: don't let the furniture get too wet, brush all of the shampoo off the upholstery thoroughly and don't let anyone sit on it until it is completely dry.

☞ Test a hidden area (e.g. hem) before cleaning to make sure colours don't run.

CANVAS: scrub with warm sudsy water; rinse in clear water. Dry in the open air. Use a soft eraser for small dirty marks.

GLAZED CHINTZ: should be dry cleaned, but you can wash it in the machine on a gentle wash and a cool rinse. Don't rub, twist, wring or bleach and, if the glaze is permanent (most modern glazes are), you should not have to starch it.

BROCADE: dry clean all brocades because they are so heavy to handle when wet.

COTTON AND LINEN: can be laundered, but be sure to remove stains before washing. If very dirty, soak in detergent or soapy suds in warm water. Wash in hot water and rinse thoroughly. Iron on the wrong side with a hot iron while fabric is still damp. If possible, starch cottons before ironing them, they will look better. Replace piped loose covers while they are still slightly damp; otherwise the piping may tighten, or even shrink.

SILK: dry clean silk taffetas and brocades. Other silks and mixtures may be very carefully washed. Iron fabric while still damp with a cool or steam iron. Clean non-removable covers with dry foam upholstery shampoo.

TWEED: dry clean woollen tweeds. Tweeds made with polyester or acrylic; these can be washed according to their fibre, check care label. Clean non-removable upholstery covers with dry foam shampoo. Don't rub wool fabric while it is wet.

VELVET: can be cotton or acrylic. If in doubt as to which fibre your velvet is made of, have it dry cleaned. Many velvets are uncrushable, spot proof and easily washed.

VELVETEEN: may be cotton or viscose, so wash as appropriate for the fibre. Shake occasionally while drying. Smooth the pile with a soft cloth. May be dry cleaned.

FURNITURE

ANTIQUE FURNITURE: dust regularly with a clean, dry duster (not feather) or chamois leather. Polish once or twice a year using an old-fashioned furniture polish. Apply sparingly and rub in well.

BAMBOO FURNITURE: brush or vacuum regularly, never use a detergent. Scrub with warm soapy water and borax. Rinse unpainted wicker and bamboo with salt water to stiffen and bleach it.

CANE FURNITURE: treat as for bamboo.

GILDED FURNITURE: dust gently with feather duster. Clean with soft cloth dipped in warm mineral turpentine or methylated spirits (warm bottle in hot water). Never rub gilding. Never let water onto the gilded surface. Never re-touch with gold paint as it will discolour.

GLASS TABLE TOP: rub with vinegar or lemon juice, dry with paper towels and buff with newspaper.

LACQUERED FURNITURE: wipe with damp cloth. Remove finger marks with damp chamois leather, rub with soft duster.

LEATHER: dust or vacuum, clean with saddle soap if necessary using little water. Allow to dry, buff with soft cloth. Rub dark leather once a year with caster oil to prevent cracking. Use petroleum jelly on pale leather. Wipe off with a soft cloth.

MARBLE: wipe regularly with a damp cloth dipped in water and mild detergent. Wipe dry and polish with a soft cloth.

MARQUETRY: dust gently. NEVER wash marquetry.

METAL: wipe occasionally with warm soapy water.

PLASTIC LAMINATE FURNITURE: don't use scouring pads or abrasive cleaners. Remove light stains with a damp cloth dipped in bicarbonate of soda.

UPHOLSTERED FURNITURE: vacuum chairs, cushions and lounge weekly. Regular dusting prolongs the life of the suite. Shampoo (with appropriate shampoo) once a year, rinse thoroughly to remove all shampoo.

WICKER FURNITURE: treat as for bamboo furniture.

WOODEN FURNITURE

CEDAR AND HARD-WOODS: remove the marks gently with steel wool, rubbing in the same direction as the wood grain.

FRENCH POLISHED FURNITURE: rub surface with clean, soft cloth. Polish occasionally with sparingly-applied furniture cream. Remove marks with a cloth dipped in warm, soapy water. Dry and polish.

MAHOGANY: dust and rub frequently. Polish furniture occasionally with light-coloured wax polish.

OAK: treat as for mahogany. Painted or varnished wood: wash with warm water and detergent, rinse and wipe dry. Don't use abrasive powders or cleaners.

PINE: treat as for mahogany.

TEAK: rub in teak oil or cream occasionally. DO NOT wax polish.

UNTREATED WOOD: unpolished or unsealed wood tables can be washed after use and dried thoroughly. Hardwood worktops or chopping boards can be rubbed with linseed oil twice a year.

VENEER: treat according to type of wood. Mop up water spills immediately.

WALNUT: treat as for mahogany.

WHITEWOOD/PLYWOOD: wipe with a damp chamois dipped in warm water. Rinse with cold water, dry. Gentle rubbing with fine, steel wool will remove stains. DO NOT scrub vigorously or use harsh abrasives.
☞ Ask about cleaning procedures when you buy the furniture!

LIGHT FITTINGS & LAMP SHADES

☞ Switch off lights at the power point and unplug lamps before you clean them.

☞ NEVER touch a live switch with wet hands.

☞ DO NOT put lampshades into water unless it's specified on the item. The fabric may be sealed with unwashable glue.

☞ DO NOT wet metal lampshade frames.

☞ Light fittings and lampshades in the kitchen and bathroom are most likely to get dirty and greasy so clean them regularly. Wash with a strong biodegradable detergent.

☞ Wipe glass bases with a damp cloth, use a toothbrush to get into any crevices. Wipe dry with kitchen paper.

☞ Dust lacquered lamp bases, do not wash.

☞ Wipe china, glazed earthenware and porcelain bases with a cloth which has been dipped in sudsy water and wrung out. Wipe dry with kitchen paper.

☞ Vacuum fabric lampshades lightly.

☞ Dust glass and metal lampshades.

☞ Wash glass and plastic lampshades, rinse well and wipe dry.

☞ DO NOT vacuum or wash paper or parchment lampshades, dust lightly with a feather duster.

☞ Have silk lampshades cleaned by a professional.

LIGHTBULBS: Clean the lightbulbs when you are cleaning the light fittings. Wipe bulbs with a damp cloth about once a month (make sure power is off!). This will make a noticeable difference to the amount of light the bulb puts out.

☞ If you remove the bulb to wipe it, make sure it is perfectly dry before you return it to the socket.

☞ Wipe fluorescent tubes with a damp cloth. Change the tubes as soon as they start to flicker.

VENETIAN BLINDS

☞ Dust each day with a clean duster.

☞ To clean fly spots and other marks, close blinds and brush with soft bristle brush. Wipe blinds down with a cloth dipped in detergent and water.

WALLS & CEILINGS

BRICK: brush and vacuum the surface occasionally. Small marks can be washed with washing soda dissolved in warm water. Rinse thoroughly. Don't get bricks too wet.

CERAMIC TILES: wash with warm water and soapless detergent, working from the top to the bottom. A cut lemon rubbed over the tiles and left for an hour will clean them. Polish with a soft cloth.

CORK: dust and vacuum. A damp cloth dipped in warm water should remove marks.

FABRIC: dust the wall and vacuum. You could try a damp cloth (in warm water) to remove marks but check first whether colour will run by testing on a hidden piece of fabric.

GLOSS PAINT: wash with warm water and soapless detergent. Add 50g borax to 1 litre of water to clean textured paint. Rinse with clean water.

NON-WASHABLE WALL PAPER: brush occasionally with a cobweb brush. Rub marks gently with a damp cloth. Pat paper dry - do not rub. A commercial cleaner is available for non-washable paper.

WASHABLE WALLPAPER: clean with a solution of detergent in warm water applied with a soft nail brush or thick cloth. Rinse thoroughly. For embossed wallpaper, apply with a soft toothbrush. Wash lacquered wallpaper with warm suds, wipe and rinse dry. Vinyl wallpaper must be dusted or damp mopped regularly. Dirt tends to make it brittle. Don't use lacquer solvents.

WATER-BASED PAINT: most marks can be washed off with detergent or soap solution. A spoonful of ammonia to the washing solution will help remove marks.

WOOD PANELLING: wipe over with a sponge rinsed in diluted detergent. Clean lacquered or varnished panelling with furniture polish.

WINDOWS

Wash glass with tepid water if windows are only slightly dirty. Dirty windows need to be scrubbed with detergent or a small amount of borax in water. A dry cloth will scratch the glass.

☞ A chamois leather is best for cleaning windows, but a linen tea-towel will do. Crumpled newspaper is good for drying them.

☞ Too much detergent causes streaks and leaves layers of residue. NEVER use soap to clean windows.

STAINED GLASS: if glass is valuable or fragile, wipe gently with a damp cloth. Don't use commercial detergent. NEVER wash painted stained glass as paint can be dislodged. Dust with a soft paint brush.

GREEN CLEANERS

If you're trying to cut down on commercial cleaners you'll be pleased to learn that most household cleaning needs can be met with seven simple ingredients: bicarbonate of soda, borax, cloudy ammonia, pure soap, strong solution ammonia, vinegar and washing soda. All are available at the local supermarket or chemist. Combinations of these substances can accomplish most household cleaning jobs cheaply and safely. Be careful with all cleaners as they may be dangerous if consumed!

BATHROOM

If you keep your bathroom well-aired it will help prevent damp and condensation, and remove odours.

☛ Wipe surfaces down with a mild biodegradable detergent solution to prevent dirt building up. Wipe toilets and basins daily.

☛ Never clean the bath or shower with abrasive cleaners.

☛ Stains can occur from leaving non-slip mats permanently in the bath or shower. Remove mats after use.

☛ Leave the shower curtain opened out after a shower to allow the air to circulate and prevent mildew.

☛ Wash canvas or cotton shower curtains in hot, soapy water. Sponge waterproof silk curtains with lukewarm suds and water on a flat surface.

☛ Air fresheners do not 'clean' the air they simply mask unpleasant odours. Home remedies are equally effective, stand a bowl of pot pourri on a window sill to scent the air. Wipe floors with vanilla.

CLEANING THE BATHROOM: for general cleaning use a firm bristled brush with either bicarbonate of soda and hot water or a mild version of the all purpose cleaner.

BATH AND SINK: use a light paste of bicarbonate of soda with water, rinse off. Rub resistant stains on acrylic baths with half a lemon.

FLOOR: for cork, lino, slate and tiles, wipe floors with cloth dipped in hot water and vinegar.

LAMINATES AND TILES: use pure soap with a plastic scourer, or make a paste of bicarbonate of soda and water and apply with a soft cloth. Wipe off paste with a clean, damp cloth.

MOULD: wipe vinegar onto the surfaces in the bathroom and leave overnight. Scrub off vinegar.

SHOWER DOORS: wipe regularly with a cloth soaked in vinegar. Clean dirt from shower door tracks with an old toothbrush.

SHOWER HEAD: unscrew the head and rub with an old toothbrush or nailbrush. Poke a bodkin or large needle through the holes to clear them. Alternatively, boil a metal shower head for 20 minutes in a solution of 1 part vinegar to 8 parts water.

SHOWER RECESS: make a paste of vinegar and washing soda to remove the soap scum.

TAPS: clean with an old toothbrush dipped in white vinegar.

TOILET: scrub the toilet bowl for a few seconds each day with a toilet brush. Rinse brush in a fresh flush of water. Wash occasionally in hot soapy water. Wash the seat, handle and cistern daily. Avoid bleach and disinfectants, use lots of elbow grease. Apply a thick paste of borax and lemon juice to stubborn areas. Leave for 2 hours, scrub and rinse off. Alternatively, pour white vinegar into the toilet bowl, let it stand 10 minutes, then scrub limescale.

WINDOWS AND MIRRORS: use ½ cup of vinegar to 1 litre of water. Rub dry with newspaper. If windows are very dirty, pre-wash with soapy water.

KITCHEN

☛ Wipe up spills immediately to prevent stains on surfaces.

☛ Wipe benchtops immediately after preparing food on them. Do not use harsh abrasive cleaners or cleaners containing bleach as they can be poisonous.

☛ Clean equipment used to prepare food as soon as possible after use to prevent bacteria forming.

☛ Clean out food cupboards about once a month because crumbs and sticky jars attract pests.

☛ Wipe sticky jars with warm soapy water. Check that all food is still fresh before returning it to the shelves.

☛ Clean out china cupboards about once a year, wash all contents before returning them to shelves.

☛ Wipe stove down with a damp sponge after cooking.

BENCHTOPS: clean with plastic scourer and soap or bicarbonate of soda. Leave a saturated cloth (with bicarbonate of soda) on caked-on spots for 10 minutes then wipe them off.

BURNT SAUCEPANS: add cold water to saucepan, add 1-2 teaspoons bicarbonate of soda, bring to the boil. Allow to cool, clean with steel wool. Alternatively, sprinkle the burnt area with salt, moisten slightly with water and leave saucepan in the sun for two days, rinse.

DRAINS: NEVER pour grease and cooking oil down the sink. A rolled up newspaper will absorb oil and can be put in the garbage. To keep drains clear, mix 1 cup bicarbonate soda, ¼ cup cream of tartar, 1 cup salt, store in a sealed jar. Once a week pour ¼ cup of the mixture into the drain. Follow with a large pot of boiling water. Keep a sink trap over the plughole to prevent food matter going into the drains and causing blockages.

CLOGGED DRAIN: pour ¼ cup bicarbonate soda followed by ½ cup vinegar. Put in the plug until the fizzing stops, then flush with boiling water. If drain remains clogged, contact a plumber. If drain is blocked with grease, try soaking with washing soda (¼ or ½ cup for hard water) and hot water.

HOTPLATES: wipe over with bicarbonate of soda on a damp cloth. Brush solid electric hotplates with a stiff wire brush.

OVEN: apply a paste of bicarbonate of soda and water to a warm oven, with a spatula, leave overnight. Clean with a stiff brush or scourer and hot water. For oven racks, soak in washing soda (¼ cup or ½ for hard water) dissolved in hot water.

REFRIGERATORS AND FREEZERS: wipe out with warm water and pure soap. Wipe down with vanilla essence or leave an open packet of bicarbonate of soda in the fridge. DO NOT use disinfectants as they taint foodstuffs.

SINK: clean with a plastic scourer and soap, or bicarbonate of soda.
Tea stains: rub mugs or cups (not delicate china) with lemon juice or salt or scour with steel wool.

WASHING DISHES: use a cake of pure soap in a wire basket, or make a lather by rubbing soap between your hands. If the water is hard, add a little washing soda to the water. In a dishwasher, use washing soda (¼ cup or ½ for hard water). Vinegar can be used in the rinse cycle to prevent streaking or spotting.

LAUNDRY

WASHING CLOTHES: dissolve soap as for washing dishes or use pure soap flakes dissolved separately in hot water. If water is hard, add washing soda.

If you have been using detergents in your laundry, it's advisable to get rid of the detergent film. To prevent yellowing, run your laundry through your machine with ⅓ cup of washing soda before you convert to soap.

SOILED NAPPIES: pre-soak nappies in 45g of bicarbonate of soda dissolved in warm water, wash in hot, soapy water, rinse and dry in the sun.

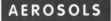

Avoid the use of aerosol products. Their production is costly in terms of the use of energy and resources. Also, aerosols use environmentally damaging propellants: chlorofluorocarbons which are detrimental to the Earth's ozone layer, and hydrocarbons which add to the smog in cities. Pump-action packs are preferable, or, in the case of personal deodorants, roll-on or solid-stick types.

CLEANING METALS

CLEANING BRASS: shine with a loose paste of vinegar and salt.

CLEANING CHROME: polish with apple cider vinegar.

CLEANING COPPER: rub with vinegar on a soft cloth. Polish with a dry cloth.

CLEANING SILVER: put a solution of one part washing soda (¼ cup or ½ cup for hard water) to 20 parts water in an aluminium pan. Dip silver in mixture briefly (bubbles are not toxic). Rinse in hot water clean thoroughly with a dry cloth.

RECYCLING

Passing on the things we no longer need (such as baby clothes), repairing broken items and buying second-hand when possible are the most obvious, immediate ways of recycling goods – and they save money in the process.

On a broader scale, there are many items which we are incapable of recycling ourselves, but which can be processed and re-fashioned to extend the life of the materials originally used to make them. Paper, glass and aluminium cans can all be recycled. Ring your local council to find out if services to collect these items from households exist in your area.

PAPER

In it's natural state, paper is a pale brown colour. To make it white, it must be bleached either by an oxygen or a chlorine process. The chlorine process, which is cheaper and more commonly used, is harmful because it creates large quantities of persistent organochlorine pollutants. These include the highly toxic chemical, dioxin, traces of which are found in items such as coffee filters, tea bags, disposable nappies and tampons.

Cutting down on your use of paper products is no great hardship.

As long as the public demands it, it will be worthwhile for companies to recycle paper products. Make sure you always use unbleached or recycled paper whenever you can find it. Ask for it in shops where you do

not see it for sale – demand creates supply.

☞ Don't waste paper. Re-use envelopes and wrapping paper. Use both sides of a piece of stationery.

☞ Use china in place of paper cups. Use cloth napkins, serviettes and handkerchiefs in place of paper ones.

☞ Disposable nappies may seem like a marvel to the busy mum, but most brands are an environmental hazard (there is a "fluff-pulp" brand that is considered less harmful). In the long-term, it is far cheaper to buy and use cloth nappies. After removing excess ex-creta, soak soiled nappies in 3 tablespoons

bicarbonate of soda dissolved in warm water. Wash in warm, soapy water. Dry outdoors when possible.

☞ Don't buy lavishly over-packaged products. Upon opening, the packaging is immediately obsolete. Remember, the land needed to dump waste is running out.

☞ If, in Australia, consumers cut back their use of paper in packaging by just 50 percent, five to nine million trees would be saved each year.

GLASS

Bottles should be recovered from con-sumers either for refilling or as cullet (smashed glass) for the manufacture of new glass containers. Although local council col-lections, bottle banks and community-based collection depots are in operation throughout the country, the majority of bottles (estimates vary between 60 and 80 per cent) are not recovered. As new glass can be comprised of 95 per cent cullet, this is a terrible waste. Don't throw away your bottles – take them to a bottle bank or make enquiries at your local council for a door-to-door collection scheme to be set up.

The system of consumers paying a deposit on soft-drinks and beer, which is refunded when the bottle is returned, has fal-len from use. It is, perhaps, time that the deposit system was reconsidered and reinstated on a national basis so that as many bottles as possible could be retrieved.

CANS

In Australia, 88 percent of cans are made of aluminium, the remainder of tin-plated steel. Recycling cans saves energy and reduces the production of carbon dioxide. Australia recycles about 56 per cent of its aluminium cans and is a world leader in this field. There are 1,100 "Cash for Can" centres nationwide, operated by Comalco and various other centres in each state. Steel cans are recycled in Sydney by Simsmetal Ltd.

☞ Avoid buying cans where possible – pur-chase fresh fruit and vegetables, and juices in bottles instead.

☞ Wash all cans thoroughly, flatten them and take them to your local collection depot. Remember: separate your rubbish into piles of those items that can be recycled. Take the recyclable material to the appropriate depot or put it out for the local council to collect. If your council does not operate a house-to-house scheme, agitate for one to be set up.

The information on environmentally friendly household cleaning methods is drawn from numerous sources including the Toxic and Haz-ardous Chemicals Committee of the Total En-vironment Centre and Greenpeace.

CARING FOR KEEPSAKES

We all have a photograph, piece of china or silver, painting or print, book or item of furniture that we treasure. It may have tremendous emotional significance, reminding the owner of a friend or relative to whom it once belonged. It may be of value in a monetary sense, or cherished simply because of its attractive appearance. Whatever its worth, taking good care of it is essential if it is to give pleasure to future generations.

While museums and art galleries always strive to exhibit works in controlled atmospheric conditions and can call upon scientific technology and the skills of professional conservators trained to repair, clean and stabilise the masterpieces in their collections, private individuals also can do a great deal to extend the life of the possessions they love. Good housekeeping practices and plenty of commonsense will go a long way to achieving this goal.

The business of cleaning old objects and repairing damage must be left firmly in the hands of the experts. Therefore, in the main, we have avoided giving "recipes" for concocting your own cleaning agents. While those given you by friends and relatives may, on the face of it, do a good job, some of the "ingredients" will put in train long-term deterioration. Time taken to consult an expert is time well spent. See the How to Find an Expert section at the end of this article. The professionals are able to analyse the composition of each object in their care and work out the best form of treatment.

Preventative conservation – that is, keeping objects in as good a condition as possible by housing them properly – is well within the reach of everyone.

NATURAL ENEMIES

We need light, heat, water and air in order to survive, but collectibles all suffer, sometimes to a devastating degree, as a result of prolonged exposure to the elements. Light fades delicate items such as watercolour paintings and fabrics; heat warps and splits wooden furniture; water causes oil paint to lift off canvases; air filled with dust particles and smoke, deposits a fine layer of grime on everything we possess.

Locking things away in a dark place is not the answer – there is little point in owning something if it's never used and enjoyed. The following tips on storage and handling will ensure that your belongings survive both the elements and the general wear-and-tear to which they are subjected.

Embroidered tablecloths, christening robes, samplers, tapestries, lace, flags and rugs are all prized as collectables. Often, each item has been worked in a variety of techniques and materials. A piece of clothing, for example, might be appliqued with different fibres that have been coloured with either natural (plant) dyes that fade fast, or modern ones that are made to last. A wall-hanging might be decorated with glued-on piping and hand-sewn with sequins, beads and metallic thread. The overall effect may be aesthetically pleasing, but there is no law of science that says all these different elements will hold together indefinitely in pristine state. Climatic conditions, insects and careless handling can all wreak havoc.

✏ Textiles are very sensitive to light. Prolonged exposure to light will fade dyes, speed up the emergence of brown ageing marks and weaken the fabric fibres. Never leave a precious textile in direct sunlight. Incandescent light bulbs should be used in preference to fluorescent tubes, and must not be pointed directly at the fabric.

✏ Don't keep textiles near food. Always make sure food particles are shaken from items such as tablecloths after use. A dirty cloth will attract insects.

✏ Moth balls and naphthalene flakes are useful in controlling insects (though not essential if you inspect your belongings regularly) but they must be used with care. Scattering them willy-nilly among the folds of a piece of textile can cause discolouration. Wrap the textile in acid-free tissue paper (available from specialist artist-supply shops) and place in a dark, but not damp, place – insects find damp spots most inviting. Put the moth balls or flakes in a little calico bag, and place alongside. Alternatively, if feasible, wrap the textile lightly around a roller. Place the calico bag of flakes inside the roller, and then cover the whole thing in acid-free tissue paper. If the tissue and roller are not acid-free, they will discolour the fabric.

✏ Never spray insect-repellent directly on to a textile. It will accelerate the degeneration process and break down the fibres.

✏ At least every three months, inspect a textile that has been stored away. Replace the moth balls if you feel you need to use them – they are not effective for ever, even if their odour does linger. If you inspect your belongings regularly, any deterioration can be quickly recognised, and dealt with by an expert.

✏ A large item that has to be folded to fit in a drawer, should be taken out occasionally, gently shaken and then refolded in a different way to prevent creases forming permanently.

✏ The humid Australian climate encourages mould. Air textiles regularly, and give large pieces, such as rugs and tapestries, a light dust with a soft brush. Don't cover framed textile with glass – it traps moisture which causes damage.

✏ Keep fabric-upholstered furniture, tapestries and wall-hangings away from smoky fireplaces, hot radiators and cigarette smoke. Heat dries, weakens and distorts fabrics; smoke leaves a stale smell and a layer of grime; burns require professional repair work.

✏ If you have a heavy wall-hanging, make sure that it is properly supported so that it won't warp or tear from its own weight. Take a hanging down occasionally and roll it on to

a tube to "rest".

☞ Whiteworks, such as lace and crochet, will turn yellow if exposed to light for long periods. Store in a dark place, wrapped in acid-free tissue paper.

☞ Never plunge an old or antique piece of fabric into water. Apart from the fact that the dyes may run (and you will have no way of knowing this until it is too late), a textile is weaker when wet. Something that seemed perfectly sound in its dry state can suddenly tear from its own weight when soaked.

☞ Never treat treasured textiles with commercial cleaning fluids. Leave cleaning, fumigation, replacement of perished materials and any other repairs and maintenance to the experts. See the How to Find an Expert column at the end of this article.

WOOD

Grandmother's beautiful kangaroo-back rocking chair and Aunt Maud's oak table need tender, loving care to keep them in good condition. Unless housed correctly, warping, splitting and fading will occur. Enjoy the different appearance and qualities that each variety of wood possesses. In recent years, this appreciation was often lacking, and the fashion for stripping wooden furniture back to base resulted in many fine pieces being spoiled. All were reduced to a bland sameness. Think carefully before you ruin the original character and value of a piece simply in order to achieve the look of the moment. Careful polishing can bring an old piece of furniture back to life, while giving it an acid bath will surely end it.

☞ In a country where temperature and humidity see-saw at an unpredictable rate, wooden furniture has a pretty hard time of it. Keep pieces away from direct sunlight, the blast of an air-conditioner and direct heat such as an open fire or radiator. Splitting and warping will result if you don't. Also, direct sunlight not only dries out wood, but will fade it – rosewood is particularly susceptible to fading. Try to maintain an atmosphere of even, mild temperature and relative humidity.

☞ Although most of them would be loath to admit it, many people are guilty of painting around the furniture when decorating, rather than taking the trouble to move large items away from the walls. However tempting, don't take this short cut. If a restorer then has to remove paint splatters from your favourite maple wardrobe, the economies of do-it-yourself home decorating are entirely lost.

☞ Dust furniture often, using a soft, clean cloth; a grubby cloth will scratch the surface of the furniture. Take care not to snag veneers or inlays.

☞ Occasionally, pieces of inlay, moulding and knobs may drop off. Don't try sticking them back on with any old glue you can find. This is a job for professionals to handle as quickly as possible. The broken piece will

soon warp or shrink, and the longer you delay attending to it, the less likely it is that it will fit back properly.

☞ If a wash-stand or chest of drawers has a marble top, clean with a feather duster, to avoid rubbing dirt into the stone. Never attempt to clean a marble top (or piece of marble sculpture) with bleach – the chlorine in the bleach will crystallise and gradually stain the marble yellow.

☞ Watch out for borers, particularly in oak, beech and walnut. Seek professional help in treating insect infestation.

☞ Never oil furniture. This will attract dirt and darken the timber. Wax once or twice a year using good-quality beeswax. Apply a thin coat and polish thoroughly. Never use a polishing agent that contains silicone because it will form a polymer on the surface of the furniture that will have to be sanded off.

✎ Careless guests can be a nightmare. Have plenty of drink coasters to hand when having a party. Rings, left by wet drinking glasses, are very hard to remove and usually need professional treatment. Better still, remove prized furniture to another room so that you don't spend the entire evening worrying about it.

CHINA AND GLASS

Porcelain, stoneware, earthenware, bone china and glass objects are probably the most visibly fragile of our possessions. Who has not smashed a cup while washing up, chipped a plate by stacking it hurriedly in the cupboard, or caused a crystal glass to cloud by absentmindedly putting it through a cycle in the dishwasher? It's not just old and antique glass and china that need looking after – a good-quality contemporary dinner service is an expensive investment and should be treated with the same care.

✎ Children and pets are hazardous creatures – don't display china or glass in areas of your home that get the most traffic. Bear in mind that a draught can topple items not securely displayed. Don't prop plates up against a wall and trust to luck – a sudden jolt will dislodge them. Make sure they are fitted carefully into a groove or specially designed stand.

✎ Never hang a cup or jug by its handle. This is its weakest point.

✎ While lack of space dictates that we stack everyday plates and dishes one on top of the other, a precious set should stand in a plate rack to avoid contact with other plates and subsequent scratching.

✎ Don't subject china and glass to sudden changes in temperature. Extreme heat and cold can make them shatter.

✎ On old china, the glaze is often worn away in places. Multiple fine cracks, known

as crazing, may also have appeared. (Extreme heat is often the culprit.) This means that the bisque layer beneath has been exposed and can easily be stained or damaged further. Never use crazed items as serving dishes for brightly coloured food such as beetroot or raspberries. Those flavoured with vegetable dyes such as saffron or curry spices should also be avoided as the cracks will absorb the colour. Similarly, never leave coffee or tea standing in a crazed container. If staining does occur, don't reach automatically for a bleach solution – it's best to seek professional advice before wrecking the piece entirely.

✎ China that is handpainted and gilded, or has lacework and ornate handles, must never go in the dishwasher. Nor should crystal or old glassware. Wash by hand using lukewarm water and a washing-up liquid that contains glycerol for degreasing. Don't use a scouring pad – it will cut through gilding, scratch the glazes and expose the bisque layer. Gilding is particularly susceptible to damage. It represents the final stage of decoration and is fired at a temperature lower than that used for the glaze; it is, therefore, less durable.

✎ Never wash ancient glass or any that is partially deteriorated.

✎ Change water in flower vases (china or glass) daily, and remove the foliage before it decays.

✎ Don't display glass in strong sunlight; apart from the heat factor, it can change the colour of the piece.

✎ In many instances, but not always, contemporary china is more durable than its older cousins. There are ranges of porcelain, for example, that are dishwasher, microwave and oven-proof. At time of purchase, check if the design you have selected has these properties. The information is usually stamped on the base of each piece.

STONE AND METAL

Because, by and large, stone and metal objects look durable, they often come in for the hardest knocks. They cannot withstand overzealous cleaning any more than a fragile painting or a piece of textile. Clean poorquality plated silver too enthusiastically and you'll start to remove the plate itself. Polish an antique bronze sculpture long and hard and you will gradually take off the patina that has taken years to build up. Patina enhances the object's visual appeal, adds to its value, and, if it is uneven, is often proof of age. (An even patina can indicate the piece is a fake.)

Further, handy recipes for concocting your own cleaning agents are often questionable in their effectiveness. What is suitable for a stone step is not necessarily ideal for a stone sculpture. Don't be tempted to experiment.! Go easy on the elbow grease at all times, and consult a professional concerning correct cleaning agents for use on your particular treasured item.

✎ In coastal regions, salt crystals from the sea settle on and erode stone surfaces, while rising damp weakens the areas it reaches. Inspect regularly and seek expert advice on conservation methods.

✎ Never clean marble sculptures with bleach; the chlorine will crystallise and gradually stain the marble an unpleasant yellow destroying the original charm.

✎ Stone sculpture that has fungus growing on it will need fumigation.

✎ Silver tarnishes easily from contact with the air with foodstuffs such as mustard, egg and salt. Fresh fruit and flowers will release damaging acids if left to stand too long in silver containers.

✎ Some commercial silver-cleaning agents are too abrasive for antique pieces. Rub it between your fingers – if it feels gritty, don't use it. A silver foam cleaner is good for intricate pieces of silver plate and sterling silver. A liquid cleaner is better for plainer items. A specially impregnated silver polishing cloth

is good for items of jewellery and cutlery, and for intricate photo frames. Always use a very soft, clean cloth when polishing or you will scratch the surface. Pewter is a particularly soft alloy – don't polish too hard.

✎ Store silverware in a dry place; warmth and moisture are its natural enemies. Wrap in acid-free tissue paper or in special cloth bags. Never use plastic wrap, as it encourages humidity and there is a danger that it will stick to the object.

✎ Metal sculptures (brass, copper, bronze) need special lacquer coatings to protect them from oxygen and sulphur. Don't lacquer fireplace equipment or anything likely to come into direct contact with fire.

✎ Ammonia is used to etch bronze – don't use it as a cleaning agent.

PAINTINGS

Few of us are fortunate enough to own a masterpiece, but a Victorian flower painting executed by a relative, a landscape of a favourite place, or a portrait of an ancestor, can be of great sentimental value. The charm of every piece should be treasured and preserved as well as possible.

Environmental pollution, insects, fluctuations in temperature, and the mix of materials that the artists themselves have used in creating their works, all play a part in the process of deterioration.

PAINTINGS ON CANVAS

✎ All paintings, whatever the medium used, need a stable environment. Unless you have air-conditioning, this may be hard to achieve. The old Australian homestead with its shady verandahs was one of the best styles of architecture for both humans and works of art – the interiors were cool and protected from shafts of searing sunlight. In a modern home, try to exhibit your paintings in a part of the house where they are least affected by the weather; you are aiming for an even, cool-to-mild temperature and relative humidity. The worst scenario is that on a damp day, when it's raining and humid, the canvas and materials will slacken. If it's hot and sunny the next day, the picture will become taut.

✎ In very dry areas of Australia, the paint surface will dessicate unless a humidifier (or bowl of water) is kept in the room.

✎ A badly aired room will encourage mould. Never place glass over an oil painting for the same reason – it traps the damp.

✎ Have fly screens fitted on windows and doors. Fly droppings have to be removed from a canvas one by one – an arduous task for a professional restorer. Never spray insect repellent on the paint surface.

✎ Water will severely damage an oil painting. The canvas will move and the paint won't. The result? The paint will be forced to "tent" up and fall off. Never wipe the surface

of an oil painting; use a feather duster only, and a very light touch.

☞ Don't hang a painting over a fireplace that is used, no matter how attractive it may look in the overall decoration of a room. Smoke ultimately discolours paint, and the heat encourages a fine crazing to develop over the painting's surface.

☞ Should you ever have to roll up a canvas, the paint layer should be on the outside. That way, it will not crack when the picture is flattened again.

☞ Don't try to clean off dirty varnish; this is a job for an expert.

WATERCOLOURS, PASTELS AND WORKS OF ART ON PAPER

Works of art on paper include maps, documents, posters, photographs, drawings and paintings, and archival material relating to your family history. For further information on the properties of paper-based memorabilia and methods of maintenance, see the Books and Photographs sections.

☞ Watercolours and pastels are even more sensitive to light than oil or acrylic paints. Bright light makes the colours fade. Unlike oil paintings, most framed works of art on paper need protecting with an ultraviolet-absorbent acrylic sheet such as Plexiglas 201 or Perspex VE. This material is also suitable as doors for bookcases and display cabinets. Glass should be used for artworks with loose media: chalk, drawings, pastels.

☞ All materials used for mounting must be acid-free. If the framer doesn't seem to know what you're talking about, go elsewhere – it's your precious belonging that's at risk. Ordinary boards and papers discolour watercolours and cause acid burn. Acid-free materials are available from specialty art-supply shops.

☞ It is false economy to have any work on paper heat-sealed cheaply onto another surface such as masonite. Once there, it is impossible to remove it or restore it. It is always better to wait until you can afford good-quality framing.

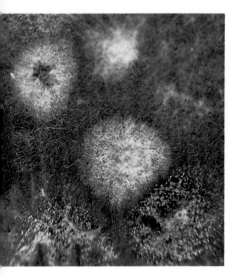

PHOTOGRAPHS

There are few more poignant reminders of the past than a faded photograph of an ancestor in their Sunday best. In these days of instant cameras, when taking colour photographs is commonplace, the old sepia and black-and-white prints have a gravity and authority that people find fascinating. Sometimes, the photographs have been hand-tinted in rather too glorious colour, while others are breathtaking in their subtlety.

Photographic material is formed from at least two layers: the image carrier (usually gelatine), and the support (usually paper or polyester). Much of the advice given for caring for works of art on paper and for books is applicable to photographs. Care for those pictures you are taking of your family today in the same way as you care for those that are 50 or more years old. They represent a valuable record of our social history.

☞ Don't leave your treasured photographs lying around in packets or boxes. The pictures at the bottom of the pile can be damaged by the weight. If you constantly sift through the box to find the picture you want, you'll cause the dust particles trapped between each one to rub against the images.

☞ Store old photographs and negatives vertically so that they bear only their own weight. Interleave the photos with polyester or polypropylene sleeves or envelopes, or neutral pH papers. Polythene can be used, but it ages faster and, in certain conditions, may stick to the photographs. Never used any plastic interleaving or form of enclosure that is made from poly vinyl chloride (PVC) as it is chemically unstable and will eventually cause the photographs to deteriorate. Suitable storage boxes, papers and protective sheeting (the types used for archival purposes by museums and libraries) are available from the S & M Supply Company Pty Ltd, which has offices in NSW, Queensland, ACT and Victoria. A comprehensive catalogue of products is available. Toll-free archival ordering and customer service (008) 02 0001. They are also available through the Museums Association of Australia.

☞ Those albums you thought were so handy – the ones with stick-down plastic film and adhesive pages to hold everything firmly in place – are not suitable for precious photographs. The chemicals in the adhesive will ultimately stain them. Also, over the years, the photos will adhere so strongly to the page that you'll need a palette knife to

lever them off. Colour photos on resin-coated paper are generally easier to remove than the older types of photographic paper – they stand the risk of being skinned in the process.

✏ Choose an album made of acid-free paper and interleave the pages as described above. Use archival-quality corner mounts or cut small diagonal slits in the pages, and insert the corners of the prints into them. Avoid albums with padded PVC covers. Never use glue to secure prints.

✏ Never clip photos together with paperclips – they can cause rust stains. Rubber bands will disintegrate and may leave permanent stains.

✏ Colour prints and slides fade fast and lose their colour balance. Keep in a cool, dark, dry place in stable conditions of humidity and temperature. Special mounting systems are available.

✏ When framing a photograph, make sure the glass or Perspex does not touch the print. It will trap the damp. There must be an acid-free window mount between the glass and the print. The backing board must also be acid-free. Never exhibit photos in direct sunlight. Colour fades fast. Ideally, use Kodachrome slide film and have Cibachrome prints made from the transparencies. These are more durable.

✏ Don't display a photograph that is showing signs of deterioration. Have it re-photographed (preferably in black-and-white) and exhibit the new print. Store the original and the new negative in a dark, dry place, in a suitable container (see information on page tc).

✏ Black-and-white photographs are more durable than colour. Consider photographing important events in black-and-white to ensure longevity.

BOOKS

The cheap paperback that we toss into our bags and briefcase is hardly in the same class as a family Bible that has been handed down through generations, or an exquisitely printed, rare First Edition. But, careless practices where cheap books are concerned can easily spill over into our treatment of publications of historical and sentimental value. Learning to care for books should begin at childhood. Folding down the corner of a page, breaking the spine, making notes in the margins and squashing too many books on the shelf at one time, are just a few of the abuses to be avoided. We are concerned with conserving both the pages themselves and the binding materials.

✏ If you've ever left a newspaper out in the sun, you know how quickly the page turn yellow and become brittle. Books suffer the same fate. Don't leave them lying open on a windowledge. The pages will dry out and the leather binding turn powdery and crumble.

✏ Books should be examined regularly to check for mould and insect infestation, then dusted and given an airing.

✏ Books should be stacked close enough together so that they are not at acute angles. Don't jam in as many books as possible as you will cause abrasion and deformation. A damp atmosphere then encourages insects and mould.

✏ Books must not overhang the shelves on which they're stored. Lay tall volumes flat on a shelf of equal or greater width.

✏ Don't store books in those areas of thehouse most affected by swings in atmospheric conditions. Hygroscopic objects (paper, textiles, wood) have an affinity for water. Very high relative humidity (greater than 65 per cent) can lead to mould growth. Low relative humidity (less than 40 percent) can cause hygroscopic material to become quite brittle.

✏ Never use sticky tape to mend a tear. It will discolour the paper, often doing irreversible damage. Professional conseravtors use acid-free glues and unbleached linen for spine linings, cords and tapes. Leave repair work to them.

✏ The edges of a book's pages will gradually become ragged. Don't put them under the guillotine to even them up. The depth of the white borders surrounding the text and illustrations is important to the overall design of the book, and, apart from the fact that trimming them is aesthetically displeasing, the value of the book can be greatly reduced. Expensive though it may be, a professional conservator can mend the edges of the pages.

✏ Treat leather bindings once a year with a dressing made of 60 per cent neat's foot oil (from saddlers) and 40 per cent anhydrous lanolin (from chemists). Mix the two together in a bowl over hot water and then store in an airtight jar. Apply a very light coating of the dressing to the leather with a soft cloth, leaving it overnight to dry. Polish off the next day with a clean, soft cloth.

✏ Books bound in vellum (a cream-coloured skin from a kangaroo, calf or goat – often used in old manuscripts) should simply be dusted. It must never get wet as it will shrink and buckle.

✏ Never spray any sort of chemical near or on a book.

CASSETTES

Store as for videos. When recording, use short-length, good-quality tapes; the longer the tape, the thinner and more fragile it is. Keep playing equipment clean. Use master tapes only to produce working tapes.

FILMS

Film is more durable than video, although initially more expensive. It may be worth having a video transposed on a film if you are particularly anxious to preserve it. Store black-and white and colour film recordings in snugly fitting canisters, vertically in racks. Keep canisters rust-free. Keep film cool, dark and dust-free. Run tapes through annually and rewind – it's important that they are evenly wound. Keep projectors clean.

VIDEOS

Keep in a dust-free atmosphere away from strong light and sudden variations in temperature and humidity. Store upright in their containers. Keep away from electric motors, TV sets and other electrical appliances to prevent the recordings being wiped. Always run tapes through to the end to prevent popular sections wearing unevenly. Keep the playing equipment clean.

HOW TO FIND AN EXPERT

Some state and regional galleries, libraries and museums hold "clinics" and workshops. Members of the public can take their collectables along for advice; check with your local gallery. When choosing a private conservator, make sure they are properly qualified. Either get a referral from a museum curator or approach the Australian Institute for the Conservation of Cultural Material (National Representative, GPO Box 1638, Canberra, ACT 2601) for a list of approved conservators. There are representatives in each state. Obtain a quote before work begins.

A mobile conservation laboratory (the only one in the world) is the brainchild of the Regional Galleries Association. The semi-trailer, with two conservators aboard, visits country towns in NSW and South Australia. Apart from cleaning and restoring paintings in the collections of the art galleries and museums, a half-day each week is set aside as a community service. This "Save it for Later" project is promoted through the National Australia Bank and information on when the unit is due is available through regional branches. To find out the laboratory's full itinerary call (02) 225 1710.

For queries concerning conservation of photographic materials, contact the Conservation Access Coordinator, State Library of NSW (02) 230 1445.

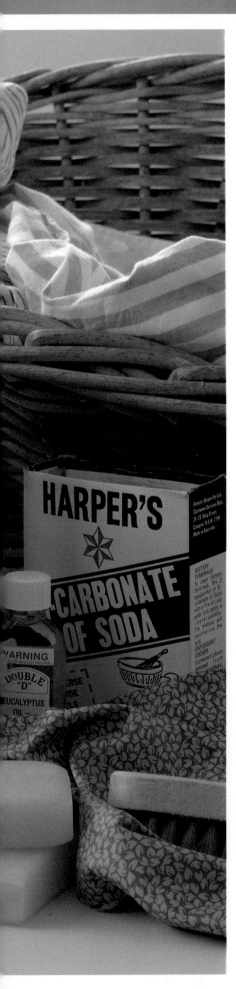

STAIN REMOVAL

The golden rule for stain removal is to treat the stain as soon as it occurs. Once it has soaked in it will be much harder to get out. Never be tempted to rub a stain, instead sponge it or scrape it. Stain removal procedures vary according to surfaces, so be sure to follow our instructions carefully. We have listed a stain removal kit for each surface, but you could easily assemble one kit for all purposes.

If you transfer cleaners into smaller, more manageable bottles or jars for your stain removal kits, be sure to label all items clearly and correctly. Do not leave the kits in any cupboard or on any shelf that is accessible to children. Remember, use caution with all cleaning agents.

Where possible, we have suggested remedies which are environmentally friendly. These make use of everyday household products such as white vinegar, salt, pure soap, lemon juice and bicarbonate of soda. Environmentally friendly tips also feature in our chapter on Cleaning.

Green heading panels denote an environmentally friendly tip.

Treat any spill as soon as it occurs – a fresh stain is more easily removed than a dried, ingrained stain.

👉 DO NOT rub or brush stains. Blot the stain, working from the outside to the centre of the stain.

👉 For liquids: pour a generous amount of salt on stain, leave an hour, then vacuum. Alternatively, blot with a wad of tissues. For solids: scrape up with the back of a knife or spatula. Do not rub in. Apply appropriate stain remover.

👉 If you begin removing a stain with one treatment, leave it to dry completely before treating other stains or using other remedies. It's only when the carpet is dry that you can see whether the stain has been removed.

👉 Rinse stain with cold water after treatment and blot dry with a clean cloth.

Specific Carpet Stains

ALCOHOL: apply diluted biodegradable detergent solution, blot dry. Apply equal parts white vinegar and water, blot dry. Rinse with cold water, blot dry.

BALLPOINT OR FELT PEN: dab gently with white spirit on a clean cloth. Shampoo with dry carpet foam.

BLOOD: apply cold water, blot. Rinse as many times as necessary, blot after each application.

BURN: on a plain light carpet, dab burn with a solution of 1 part hydrogen peroxide to 10 parts water.

CANDLE WAX: place one or two layers of brown paper or paper towels over wax, press with hot iron. Paper will absorb the wax. Repeat with clean paper until wax is gone. If stain is from coloured candle wax, dab with methylated spirits. Repeat process until stain is removed.

COFFEE, BLACK: spray with soda siphon or splash with soda water, blot. Shampoo with dry carpet foam.

Stain Removal Kit – Carpets

Assemble the following items in a tool box, basket or shoe box. Label each item clearly and keep the contents out of the reach of children.

Clean cloths
(preferably absorbent towelling)

Brown paper or paper towelling

Detergent *(biodegradable)*

Dry-cleaning fluid *(optional)*

Dry foam carpet shampoo

Eucalyptus oil *(optional)*

Household ammonia
(must be diluted before use)

Methylated spirits

Mineral turpentine

Salt

Soft-bristled brush

White tissues

COFFEE, WHITE: spray with soda siphon or splash with soda water, rinse, blot. Shampoo with dry carpet foam. If milk stain remains, dab with mineral turpentine and dry-cleaning fluid, sponge with a mixture of 1 teaspoon each of white vinegar and biodegradable detergent in 1 litre warm water.

CRAYON: dab with mineral turpentine. Sponge with a solution of 1 litre warm water containing 1 teaspoon each of white vinegar and biodegradable detergent.

CREAM, ICE-CREAM, MILK: apply a small amount of biodegradable liquid detergent solution to stain, rinse with cold water.
☛ Dab with mineral turpentine or dry-cleaning fluid, shampoo with dry carpet foam.
☛ Sponge with a mixture of 1 teaspoon each of white vinegar and biodegradable detergent in 1 litre warm water.

FAECES: remove deposit, sponge with clear, warm water, spray with soda siphon or splash with soda water. Disinfect, shampoo.

FELT TIP PEN: treat as for BALLPOINT PEN.

FRUIT JUICE: blot stain with a cloth dipped in a mild solution of biodegradable detergent and water. Shampoo if necessary.

FURNITURE POLISH: dab with mineral turpentine or dry-cleaning fluid on cotton wool, sponge with a solution of 1 litre warm water containing 1 teaspoon each of white vinegar and biodegradable detergent.

ICE-CREAM: treat as for CREAM.

MILK: treat as for CREAM.

MUD: leave to dry, brush or vacuum. Dab stain with methylated spirits, then liquid detergent solution, rinse. Repeat process if necessary.

PAINT: most paint stains CANNOT be removed once they are dry.
Acrylic: sponge out with diluted biodegradable detergent, dab with methylated spirits.
Gloss: sponge with methylated spirits or mineral turpentine if paint is wet.
Water-based: sponge out with cold water while still wet.

SOFT DRINK: apply diluted biodegradable detergent solution, blot dry. Apply a mixture of equal parts white vinegar and water, blot, rinse with cold water.

SHOE POLISH: scrape off as much residue as possible. Dab with mineral turpentine or dry-cleaning fluid.
☛ Sponge with a solution containing 1 teaspoon each of white vinegar and biodegradable detergent.

TEA, BLACK, TEA, WHITE: treat as for COFFEE, BLACK, COFFEE, WHITE.

URINE: sponge immediately with cold water, blot with a solution of equal parts white vinegar and water. Rinse, blot dry. Shampoo if necessary.

VOMIT: scrape up deposit. Sponge with a solution of 1 litre warm water containing 1 teaspoon each of white vinegar and biodegradable detergent.

WINE, RED: sprinkle generously with salt, leave overnight, vacuum. Shampoo.

WINE, WHITE: sponge with a solution of 1 litre warm water containing 1 teaspoon each of white vinegar and detergent.

As with all stains, treat immediately. If the stain is not greasy and the garment is washable, put it straight into cold water. Hot water "cooks" the stain and fixes it. A stain will come out more easily if it is removed the way it went in, so work from the back of the fabric through to the front.

Soaking
Soaking garments before you wash them will get rid of stubborn dirt. You may need to soak some stains for 12 hours or more in a biodegradable detergent solution. DO NOT soak them in a metal container, it may rust, use plastic.
☛ Make sure the laundry powder is dissolved before adding garments.
☛ NEVER soak woollens, silks, leather, drip-dry or non-colourfast fabrics or fabric with a flame-proof finish.
☛ NEVER soak coloureds and whites together as colours may run.
☛ NEVER soak metal zippers or metal clasps in detergent; they can rust.
☛ Be patient! A long soak is often more effective than a thorough wash.

Bleaching
Residual stains can be bleached, BUT be sure to follow these guidelines if you are using bleach.
☛ ALWAYS wear rubber or plastic gloves when bleaching fabric.

☛ Check the care label to see if bleaching is suitable. If unsure, dab a weak solution on a hidden part of the garment, for example, the hem.
☛ NEVER use undiluted chlorine bleaches as they will burn holes in the fabric.
☛ NEVER USE chlorine bleach on wool, silk, rayon, deep-coloured or drip-dry cottons or cottons with finishes.
☛ Rinse fabric THOROUGHLY after bleaching.
☛ Don't wash unbleached fabrics with clothing that has been soaking in bleach as the bleach may affect the unbleached fabric.
☛ Hydrogen peroxide can be used on wool or silk. Mix 1 part hydrogen peroxide to 4 parts cold water. Soak item for up to 12 hours, rinse thoroughly.

Stain Removal Kit – Fabrics

Absorbent cotton material
(*put behind stain to absorb surface liquid*)

Bicarbonate of soda

Borax

Cotton wool

Clothes brush

Detergent *(biodegradable)*

Eye dropper or syringe
(*for use of strong solvents*)

Glycerine

Household ammonia

Hydrogen peroxide

Lemons
(*the juice is a valuable stain remover*)

Methylated spirits

Plastic spray bottle
(*to spray stains*)

Pure soap

Sandpaper

Small, clean sponges

White vinegar

☞ Chlorine bleach can be used on small stains or spots on cotton or linen. Mix 10ml bleach with 800ml cold water, dab stain with cloth moistened in the solution, rinse, wash as normal. For larger stains, immerse garment in solution of 500ml bleach to 8 litres water, leave 10 minutes, check stain, leave few minutes longer if necessary. Do not leave more than 15 minutes. Rinse, wash.

Specific Fabric Stains

ACIDS: immediately plunge into cold water. Dab on bicarbonate of soda dissolved in cold water, rinse thoroughly.

ADHESIVES: *cellulose-based:* wash out in cold water, or wet and treat with diluted household ammonia.
Epoxy adhesive: remove with methylated spirits before glue sets.
PVA: dab with methylated spirits to remove.
Sticky labels/adhesive tape: soak in water, or sponge with methylated spirits.

BALLPOINT PEN: if ink is fresh, sprinkle with salt, remove stained salt and apply fresh batches until stain is removed.

☞ If ink is dry, dab with methylated spirits and sponge with warm water containing 1 teaspoon each of biodegradable liquid detergent and white vinegar.

BEER: soak garment in white vinegar, rinse, wash in hot water containing biodegradable liquid detergent.

BEETROOT: sponge immediately with cold water, soak in cold water overnight. Sponge with biodegradable liquid detergent, rinse.

BLOOD: wash immediately in cold water containing salt, rinse. Do not use warm or hot water.
☞ For hardened stains, soak in cold water containing biodegradable liquid detergent. Household bleach can be used if fabric is suitable.

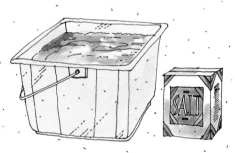

BLOOD: soak in cold water for 10 minutes, wash with pure soap.

BUTTER: remove excess butter. Wash fabric at high temperature, using a biodegradable detergent.

CANDLEWAX: place the fabric between brown or blotting paper, rub a warm iron over paper to melt wax. Dab the stain with methylated spirits.

CHEWING GUM: dab with ice cubes to freeze gum or place in freezer, break gum off. Treat remaining stain with methylated spirits.

CHOCOLATE: scrape off chocolate, rinse in cold water, soak and wash in hot, soapy water.

COCOA: sponge with glycerine, leave three to four hours, wash with pure soap and cold water.

COFFEE: soak in a solution of bio-degradable detergent and warm water, dab stain with methylated spirits.
➡ Wash off milky coffee in warm water containing biodegradable detergent.

COFFEE: wash immediately in cold water, then white vinegar, rinse.

CORRECTION FLUID: *white water-based:* wash with warm water and pure soap. *White-solvent based:* dab stain with a cloth dipped in mineral turpentine. Sponge gently with damp sponge and a little liquid detergent to remove turpentine.

CRAYON: dab with methylated spirits, rinse well.

CREAM: scrape off excess cream, rinse in cold water. Soak fabric in water containing biodegradable detergent or borax.

CURRY POWDER: soak in diluted household ammonia, rinse, wash as normal. Bleach stain if fabric is suitable.
➡ If fabric is non-washable dab with a solution of borax and water or ammonia and water.

DEODORANT: sponge with bio-degradable liquid detergent, wash in hot water. If stain persists, dab with dry-cleaning fluid, then household ammonia, rinse.

DYES: rinse in cold water, dab with biodegradable liquid detergent. If stain remains, dab with methylated spirits.

EGG: rinse in cold water, wash with biodegradable liquid detergent.

ENGINE OIL: sponge with undiluted liquid detergent. If stain persists, dab with dry-cleaning solvent.

FAECES: scrape off deposit. Soak in a borax solution for half an hour. Wash as normal with pure soap.

FAT: if fat has dried, treat as for BUTTER. If fat is hot, sponge with biodegradable liquid detergent, rinse.

FELT TIP PEN: sponge with glycerine or pure soap, wash normally. Sponge any residue with methylated spirits.

FOUNDATION CREAM: sponge with bio-degradable liquid detergent, wash fabric out in water.

FRUIT & FRUIT JUICE: sprinkle salt over stain, rinse in cold water, soak in biodegradable liquid detergent. Wash at high temperature. Treat any residual stain with diluted hydrogen peroxide or borax.

FRUIT: immediately cover with salt, soak in milk, wash as normal.

GLUES: treat as for ADHESIVES.

GLUES: many glues can be removed by dabbing with eucalyptus oil.

GRASS STAIN: dab with methylated spirits. Dry fabric, wash with biodegradable liquid detergent.

GRAVY: soak in cold water or biodegradable detergent.

GREASE: scrape off excess. Wash at high temperature using washing soda and borax. Hydrogen peroxide will also dissolve grease. Treat residual stain with dry-cleaning fluid.

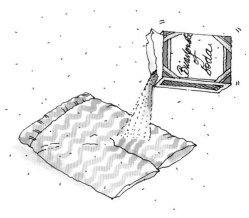

GREASE: if stain is fresh, sprinkle thickly with bicarbonate of soda, leave a few minutes, brush off.
➡ For dried grease, wet fabric and rub bicarbonate of soda into stain, wash fabric as normal.
➡ Alternatively, dampen a cloth with eucalyptus oil and dab onto stain, wash as normal.

HONEY: scrape off excess, rinse in cold water, wash in biodegradable detergent. If stain remains, dab with hydrogen peroxide.

ICE CREAM: remove excess with a spoon or knife. Soak garment in warm water containing biodegradable detergent.

INK: if ink is still wet, wash with cold water, sponge with biodegradable liquid detergent or lemon juice, rinse garment with household ammonia.

INK: soak in milk.

IODINE: sponge with methylated spirits or wash in warm soapy water and leave in the sun to dry.

JAM: rinse in cold water, soak in biodegradable liquid detergent. If stain persists, sponge with diluted hydrogen peroxide.

LIPSTICK: dab with methylated spirits, wash in biodegradable liquid detergent containing about 3 drops of household ammonia.

LIPSTICK: sponge stain gently with bicarbonate of soda mixed with lemon juice before washing.

LIQUEURS: rinse in cold water, wash in biodegradable liquid detergent.

MEAT JUICE: rinse in cold water, soak in biodegradable detergent.

MILDEW: soak in a weak solution of warm water and household ammonia, or sponge with white vinegar.

● Wipe mildewed leather with antiseptic mouthwash.

MILDEW: the fungus can be killed by hanging fabric in hot sun or outside on a frosty night.

MILK: rinse in cold water, soak in biodegradable detergent.

MUD: brush off when dry. Dab residual stain with methylated spirits, followed with biodegradable liquid detergent.

MUSTARD: rinse in cold water, soak in biodegradable liquid detergent.

MUSTARD: sponge with glycerine, leave three to four hours, wash with pure soap and cold water.

NAIL VARNISH/POLISH: flush with methylated spirits, wash. DO NOT treat with oily nail varnish remover.

OIL: treat as for GREASE

PAINT: *acrylic:* blot with tissues, wash in detergent, or dab with methylated spirits.
Oil-based: sponge with methylated spirits, soak in biodegradable liquid detergent.

PERFUME: dab with household ammonia straight from the bottle, wash in biodegradable liquid detergent.

PERFUME: sponge with glycerine, leave three to four hours, wash with pure soap and cold water.

PERSPIRATION: if stains are old, sponge with a solution of water and 1 teaspoon vinegar. If stains are fresh, wash as normal.

RASPBERRY: wash with soapy water, rub with lemon juice, leave stain an hour before washing.

RUST: sprinkle stain with salt, dab with lemon juice, wait five minutes and repeat if necessary.
● Saturate stain with lemon juice, cover with bicarbonate of soda, leave to soak, rinse mixture off.

RUST: saturate with lemon juice, rub with salt and leave in direct sunlight until dry. Wash as normal.

SCORCH MARK: dampen stain with a solution of 1 part glycerine to 2 parts water, rub in with fingertips. Soak in a solution containing 50g borax to 600ml water. Leave 15 minutes. Wash as normal.

SCORCH MARK: sponge with white vinegar, rinse with cool water.

SHOE POLISH: sponge with methylated spirits, rinse, wash.

SOFT DRINKS: rinse in cold water, soak in biodegradable liquid detergent. If stain persists, sponge with methylated spirits diluted with a little white vinegar.

TEA: soak in warm biodegradable detergent and water, dab with methylated spirirts.

TEA: sponge with glycerine, leave three to four hours, wash with pure soap and cold water.

TOBACCO: rinse in cold water, then in white vinegar. Wash in biodegradable liquid detergent containing a little methylated spirits. If stain persists, dab with diluted hydrogen peroxide.

TOMATO SAUCE: rinse in cold water, soak in biodegradable liquid detergent. If stain remains, dab with methylated spirits.

URINE: sprinkle salt generously on stain until urine is absorbed, rinse in cold water. If stain persists, sponge with household ammonia straight from the bottle, rinse, sponge with white vinegar. Wash with a biodegradable detergent.

VEGETABLE OIL: wet fabric with cold water, sponge with methylated spirits containing a little white vinegar.

VOMIT: scrape off excess. Spray with a soda siphon or splash with soda water, sponge with a borax solution or soak in biodegradable detergent.

WATERMARK: on silk, rayon or wool, cover spout of kettle (containing boiling water) with muslin and hold stain over the steam until stain is damp, but not wet. Shake off excess dampness, iron stain.

WAX POLISH: sponge with dry-cleaning fluid, wash in biodegradable liquid detergent.

WINE: cover immediately with salt. Soak in cold water or a borax solution for half an hour. Wash as normal.

WINE: cover immediately with salt or hot water, soak in milk, wash as normal.

Bio-degradab

WASHING
SODA
500g NET

Non-pollut

Made & Packed by JAMES HUNTE
1 Ivy Street, Botany,
Phone 666 8566

STORE IN A COO

If treating a stain with water or other liquids, test a hidden piece of wallcovering to make sure the colours won't run.

BRICK

GRAFFITI: sponge with paint remover, allowing time for it to work before you scrape it off. Wash with biodegradable detergent solution.

👉 If you can't bear the marks and no remover works, try gently sandpapering off the graffiti.

GREASE: sponge with methylated spirits or any white spirit.

UNIDENTIFIED SPOT: wash with warm biodegradable detergent solution containing about ½ cup washing soda, rinse well.

CORK

GREASE: dab with water containing borax, or a solution of mild biodegradable household detergent containing a few drops of household ammonia.

INK: blot immediately and try not to smear. Dab with methylated spirits.

PENCIL: rub gently with a pencil eraser.

UNIDENTIFIED SPOT: sponge carefully with warm water and detergent. Do not get cork too wet.

WAX CRAYON: place brown or blotting paper over stain, press with warm iron. If colour remains, sponge with methylated spirits or bicarbonate of soda on a moistened cloth.

PAINT

ADHESIVE TAPE: peel off while still fresh. If tape is old, dab with non-oily nail varnish

Stain Removal Kit – Walls
Blotting paper
Clean absorbent cloths
Detergent *(mild, biodegradable)*
Household ammonia
Methylated spirits
Mineral turpentine
Pencil eraser
Sandpaper
Sponges
Talcum powder
Washing soda

remover to soften glue, then carefully peel off. Don't leave varnish remover on too long as it will damage some paint. If paint lifts, touch up with new paint.

BALLPOINT PEN: sponge stain with methylated spirits.

FELT TIP PEN: can be removed with biodegradable detergent. If stain remains, a new coat of paint may be the only solution.

GREASE: sponge with strong biodegradable detergent solution containing a little methylated spirits or household ammonia.

UNIDENTIFIED SPOT: *oil-based paint*: dust, wash with detergent. Rub residual stain with a cut lemon.
Water-based paint: dust, wash with weak detergent solution, rinse and dry.
Plaster: treat as for BRICK.

WALL COVERINGS

ADHESIVE TAPE: sponge area with methylated spirits, rinse, dry.

GREASE: *embossed:* dab with talcum powder, leave a few hours, brush off.
Hessian: dab with methylated spirits after testing for colour fastness.
Silk: seek professional advice for all stains.
Vinyl: dab with methylated spirits or any white spirit, then dab stain with detergent solution.
Washable and Unwashable: place brown or blotting paper over stain and press with warm iron.
☛ Moistened borax on the residual stain may help remove it.
☛ Apply a thick paste of talcum powder and dry-cleaning fluid over the stain, rub gently, allow to dry then brush off. May need to be applied two or more times.

INK: blot ink immediately and try not to smear it. Dab with methylated spirits.

PENCIL: rub gently with a pencil eraser.

UNIDENTIFIED SPOT: *embossed:* rub with soft eraser.
Hessian: dab with talcum powder, leave about two hours, brush off. Don't use dry-cleaning or upholstery fluids.
Textured: sponge with a mild detergent solution.
Vinyl: dab with weak detergent solution, rinse well.
☛ Rubbing with a cut lemon may remove residual stain.
Washable and Unwashable: rub with stale bread rolled into a ball. Do not wet the wallcovering.

WAX CRAYON: place brown or blotting paper over stain, press with warm iron.
☛ Sponge any colour stain remaining with methylated spirits or bicarbonate of soda on a damp cloth.

WOOD PANELLING
Any treatment will discolour the wood so you will need to stain or polish it to regain colour.

GRAFFITI: sponge with mild biodegradable detergent solution, dab with methylated spirits.

UNIDENTIFIED SPOT: if sealed, sponge with mild biodegradable detergent solution, rinse. If wax finished, polish with furniture polish.

WOOD FURNITURE

Wipe up spills immediately and never apply much water to the furniture.

ADHESIVES: remove adhesive before it dries, rub stain with smooth peanut butter or vegetable oil, polish with clean cloth.

ALCOHOL: soak up immediately, wipe with furniture polish or linseed oil, depending on type of wood.

BLOOD: soak up immediately. Blood is unlikely to stain treated wood.
☛ If stain occurs on natural wood, sandpaper the surface lightly and dab with hydrogen peroxide.

CIGARETTE BURN: treat as for HEAT MARK below.

COFFEE or TEA: wipe up immediately. Treat as HEAT MARK below.

COSMETICS: treat as for ALCOHOL.

FAT: treat as for GREASE.

GREASE: remove stain with lighter fluid. For veneered or inlaid wood, cover stain thickly with talcum powder, cover with layers of kitchen towelling, press carefully with warm iron.

HEAT MARK, WHITE: remove finish with methylated spirits. When dry, recolour wood with suitable wood stain or polish. Repolish whole surface.
☛ For lacquered finishes, rub with brass polish, wipe off polish before it dries, rub with clean cloth heated in oven. Repolish.

SCRATCHES: *ebony*: rub scratch with matching wax crayon, eyebrow pencil or black shoe polish.
Mahogany: rub with matching wax crayon, eyebrow pencil or dark brown shoe polish.
Maple: rub with iodine diluted with methylated spirits, dry, rewax.
Oak: rub with white or pale brown shoe polish, rewax.
Pine: treat as for OAK.
Teak: sandpaper gently, rub with a solution of equal parts linseed oil and turpentine.
Walnut: rub with broken walnut kernel.

WATERMARK, WHITE: rub stain with fine steel wool and oil in direction of grain. Apply a paste of olive oil and cigarette ash or oil and salt. Buff with damp cloth.

WATERMARK, BLACK: rub stain with fine steel wool until fresh wood appears. Re-stain or re-polish as necessary.

HEAT MARK, BLACK: rub with cut lemon to bleach mark, repeat if necessary. Treat as for HEAT MARK, WHITE.

INK: soak up ink immediately with a damp cloth. Rub stain with cut lemon.

MILK: treat as for ALCOHOL.

OIL: treat as for GREASE

PAINT: dry paint is difficult to remove, so tackle the stain as soon as it happens.
Oil-based: wipe with turpentine, polish.
Water-based: wipe with solution of water and pure soap, wipe dry, polish.

Information for green tips supplied by the Toxic and Hazardous Chemicals Committee of the Total Environment Centre and Greenpeace.

HOUSEHOLD PESTS

Household pests can drive you to distraction, or that can of heavy duty insecticide! In this chapter you'll find a variety of remedies which are simple, efficient and friendly to you and the environment. If at any time you need to use an insecticide, remember these points:

☞ Follow the instructions carefully and if any gets on your skin, wash it off immediately.

☞ Don't spray any insecticide near elderly people or food.

☞ Don't use insecticides containing chlorofluorocarbons as they are harmful to the environment; pump action pumps are preferable.

Remember, the easiest way to discourage pests setting up residence is to keep all surfaces clear of food scraps and clutter, to keep rubbish bins clean and disinfected and to vacuum thoroughly and frequently.
If you are plagued by a particular pest, seek help from a professional pest exterminator.

SAFETY

☞ Keep all pesticides and baits locked up away from children at all times.

☞ Remove dead mice that have been poisoned immediately so that pets don't eat them.

ANTS

The best way to deter ants is to keep all surfaces clean, but if they persist, try one of these methods.
☞ To keep them away, rub pennyroyal oil on shelves or add a few drops of water and spray the area. ·

Ground cloves in the corners of cupboards or a cut lemon can also deter ants.

Cotton wool soaked in paraffin and put near the entrance of the ants nest (if you can locate it) may encourage them to move elsewhere.

Place cucumber ends or sprinkle eucalyptus oil around the area.

Sprinkle around peppermint or spearmint leaves.

Ants will also retreat from lines of talcum powder, chalk and cayenne pepper.

These methods do not kill the ants, so if you feel you need a more long-term solution, try a sweet bait: mix 600ml water, 60g borax and 60g boracic acid. Heat to make a syrup. Soak cotton wool in syrup, place in small plastic bag with a hole cut in corner; this allows the ants to get in. Leave in an area where the ants frequent.

BEDBUGS

Bedbugs can be found in old and new homes – mattresses, door and window frames, skirting boards or even behind wallpaper. Spray the infested area/s thoroughly with an insecticide containing pyrethrum, malathion or lindane. Air the room thoroughly before sleeping in it. If bugs persist, call in the fumigators. Try to avoid the highly toxic organoclorines still being used by many pest control firms. There are alternatives so ask about the chemicals they will use.

COCKROACHES

Sprinkle affected areas with pyrethrum powder or oil.

Place cucumber ends in cupboards, leave until they are dead and shrivelled. Remove, replace with fresh cucumber ends.

Sprinkle boracic acid in cupboards, or try a mixture of powdered borax and sugar or dust borax around fridge and stove area.

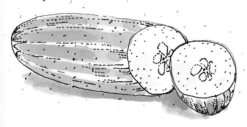

Place a mixture of 5 percent borax in sugar in a milk bottle top or similar container and leave out as a bait.

Eucalyptus oil can be used as an insecticide against cockroaches. Sprinkle around cupboards and corners.

Place a beer-soaked rag in a shallow dish and leave overnight.

FLEAS

Vacuum the area thoroughly – carpet, under rugs, skirting boards, curtains, upholestry, any warm place where fleas may lurk. Flea eggs can hatch in 2 to 12 days if it's warm, or can lay dormant for months in cool weather. Burn the contents of the vacuum cleaner. Vacuum frequently. If your pet has fleas, throw away or wash the bedding, replace it with disposable paper or the like until the fleas are gone. Treat the pet with appropriate powder or wash.

Treat room with Fleaproof fogger which contains permethrin to kill the fleas, and Methoprene which prevents fleas from growing up from further hatchings.

Eucalyptus oil sprinkled around affected areas can deter fleas.

For pets, use shampoo containing pyrethrin, or natural insect repellants such as peppermint oil or citronella (available from chemists). Comb the pet frequently with a fine flea comb.

If you are unsure about how to treat your pet, or if your pet won't take any treatment seek advice from a vet. Some treatments may aggravate the animal.

FLIES

Install fly screens.

Crushed mint on the kitchen bench deters flies.

Leave a few camphor tablets on or near your kitchen bin.

Place bay leaves on window sills or pantry shelves.

Leaves of lavender, pennyroyal or rue in a vase or hung up also deters flies – rub the leaves frequently to release the scent.

Small pots of tansy also deter flies.

A pot of growing basil in the kitchen will keep the flies away.

Make sticky paper (honey on yellow paper) to catch flies.

LICE

Head lice eggs are small, white and regular in shape. They attach firmly to a child's hair, behind the ears and along the nape of the neck. It's a common condition among school children and can be treated easily.

Wash the child's hair with a special shampoo available from chemists. Apply shampoo as per instructions and remove the lice with a fine tooth comb. Wash all the child's hair combs, brushes, ribbons, headbands, pillowcases and sheets.

Thoroughly vacuum all furniture, particularly headrests of chairs and sofa, and all carpets and rugs to remove any eggs. Burn contents of vacuum cleaner.

MICE

Keep all food packed in metal or glass.

Hang sprigs of mint or tansy in kitchen cupboards, rub them frequently to release their scent. Pots of mint in the kitchen are also a deterrent.

- Oil of peppermint rubbed around the area you suspect they inhabit will deter them.
- Traps are effective. Use lightly cooked bacon, peanut butter or cheese as baits. Rats have a taste for brazil nuts. Check traps regularly and dispose of the dead mice.

MOSQUITOES

Mosquitoes breed in water, so it's a good idea to get rid of any puddles of still water lying around you house and make sure water doesn't build up in gutters or downpipes.
- Baby oil, citronella, castor oil or lavender oil rubbed on skin are natural repellents.
- To repel mosquitoes use mozzie zappers, incense, citronella or pyrethrum candles, pyrethrum, mosquito nets or coils.
- Pots of basil discourage mosquitoes.

MOTHS

Moths tend to lay eggs in cotton, woollen and fur materials which will provide food for the larvae when they hatch. To avoid this, make sure all clothes, linen and fabrics are clean before you store them. Clean out cupboards and wardrobes occasionally and check for signs of moths. Clothes that you wear frequently are often not affected by moths.
- Wipe clothes drawers out with a solution

of 1 part ammonia to 5 parts water.
- Store blankets, quilts, curtains and clothes in sealed polythene bags in an airtight container.
- Dried wormwood, tansy, lavender, whole cloves or cedar wood shavings amongst clothes deters moths. Place them in gauze sachets and scatter through clothes.
- Moth-proof blankets by melting a block of camphor in the last wash.
- Dried orange peel scattered through clothing will deter moths.
- Make up muslin bags containing 50g of black pepper, cinnamon, ground cloves and orris root (available from chemists and health-food shops) and place them throughout drawers.

PLANT PESTS

- Control house-plant pests by spraying plants with a solution of warm water containing hot pepper.
- Wash plants with soap and water, rinse thoroughly afterwards.

SILVERFISH

- Sprinkle Epsom Salts or coarse salt in corners or drawers, wardrobes and rooms.

- Cut cloves of garlic on shelves also deter silverfish.
- Cloves or a lavender bag amongst clothes will deter silverfish.
- Make a trap with 1 part molasses to 2 parts vinegar. Leave in corners etc.

SNAILS/SLUGS

- Pick the snails up at night after rain or watering, and discard.
- A saucer with beer in it attracts snails, but it should be emptied the next day.
- Blue-tongue lizards dispose of snails and slugs.
- Broken eggshells, sawdust and wood ash act as physical barriers and so discourage them.

TERMITES

Organise a regular inspection by a qualified operator. If you find termites, have them identified – not all species are pests.
- Reduce the likelihood of an attack by ensuring building timbers and sub floor are dry and well ventilated.
- Damaged wood should be removed. Seek the advice of a pest control operator. Again, try to avoid the highly toxic organochlorines, there are alternatives.

WASPS

If it's a bad infestation of wasps, call in professionals to deal with the nest. Wasps can be quite dangerous if they are aggravated. If you have no choice but to deal with the nest yourself, buy an appropriate insecticide and follow the instructions carefully. The insecticide is likely to be poisonous to you as well as the wasps. Wear rubber gloves and even protective clothing while spraying. Keep the insecticide out of the reach of children at all times!

WEEVILS

- Always store food in sealed, airtight containers.
- Sprinkle a little cooking salt around food shelves.
- A bay leaf in dry food containers will deter food moths and weevils from laying eggs.
- Hang small cloth sacks of black pepper in bean and grain containers.

REPAIRS & MAINTENANCE

Housekeeping in the broadest sense goes well beyond the realms of everyday cooking and cleaning. A house needs to be serviced in much the same way as a car and you can do a major part of this general servicing. Only the rarest and keenest individuals set aside specific times to clear the gutters and test walls for damp; the more common approach is to attend to things as problems occur. But there is good sense in being prepared in advance, especially in the case of gutters, because a gushing overflow in the midst of a downpour indicates that leaves are blocking a down pipe and it is preferable by far to fix the problem on a fine day before this happens than in rain and, as luck usually has it, the dark as well.

It is best to be aware that things can go wrong and check possible problem areas regularly. A practical person with steady hands, who is also endowed with commonsense, can undertake all kinds of household repairs and maintenance tasks.

However, the home handyperson should exercise restraint and discretion when dealing with repairs to the services and appliances which bring gas, electricity and water into the home; check first and find out about relevant laws in your area. Although regulations are often strict to the point where authorities in some areas forbid anyone other than a licensed electrician to carry out any electrical work, or state that only a licensed plumber is entitled to change the washer on a tap, the reasons behind these rules are protection of the consumer and protection of the service.

If there appears to be a major problem which is beyond your capabilities or which would involve you in breach of the law, switch off the relevant services at the mains, reach for the telephone and call in professional tradespeople.

THE BASIC TOOL KIT

Good quality tools more than repay you with efficiency and long life, so don't scrimp when assembling your basic tool kit. If there are some items which just keep disappearing because of their desirability factor to other members of the household (a craft or blade knife for instance is frequently a missing tool), have a back up supply in a secret place so you won't be inconvenienced by someone else's thoughtless action.

1. ADJUSTABLE SPANNERS: in a couple of sizes for plumbing work and for adjusting nuts on bolts.

2. BRADAWL: for making holes in timber before drilling and also ideal for piercing leather. A gimlet has a screw-like end instead of the sharp point of the bradawl.

3. CHISELS: in two sizes, large and small, for making cavities in timber. Keep them sharp, store them on the wall or with their blades wrapped in cloth, and never use them as screwdrivers.

4. COPING SAW: with replaceable blades, is perfect for cutting curves and intricate shapes. An essential tool for making dolls furniture.

5. CLAW HAMMER: for pulling out as well as

Tool Box Notions

Adhesives (*rubber, PVA and epoxy resin glue)*

Adhesive tape

Brown plastic packaging tape

Insulating tape

Nails, screws and picture hanging hardware

knocking in nails. Remember to hold it properly by the end of its handle, and not up near its head, so you can make each blow effective and also avoid scorn of onlookers.

6. FILE: for smoothing timber corners and edges.

7. G-CLAMPS: for anchoring timber to

workbench. Useful for clamping joints and laminations during construction.

8. HACKSAW: with removable blades for cutting through pipes and cables. Replace blades frequently.

9. HAND DRILL: quaintly old-fashioned but still very useful and gives the operator much

better control than a power drill. Ideal for small jobs.

essential companion of the tenon saw and used for setting the saw blade at exactly 90 or 45 degrees.

used for recessing nails into timber.

also called a crosscut saw, for timber and timber derivative materials such as chipboard and hardboard. Definitely not for metal. Keep it oiled to prevent rust and store in a dry place.

for finishing timber. Adjust the blade to alter the depth of the cut. The blade

can also be removed from the plane, chisel and knife blades.

for straightening, bending, gripping and removing nails and cutting wire. With insulated handles, pliers are suited to electrical work. A wire stripper is also useful for electrical repairs and needle-nosed pliers can reach into awkward places.

15. RETRACTABLE KNIFE: for cutting cardboard, vinyl and cork and making fine adjustments in cuts in timber.

16. SCISSORS: for cutting paper and twine. Keep a cheap pair in the tool box to discourage misuse of dressmaking scissors.

17. SCREWDRIVERS: have them in a variety of sizes. The tiny one which comes with the sewing machine is often useful around the house – ensure that it is always returned to its rightful place. Phillips-head screwdrivers must fit Phillips-head screws or they will slip, so buy a selection of sizes.

18. SPIRIT LEVEL : ensures that surfaces are precisely vertical or horizontal and will also settle disputes about crooked pictures.

19. SQUARE: for marking out right angles. A combination square has a built in spirit level and also makes it possible to mark out 45 degree angles.

20. STEEL TAPE : which is flexible and retractable. Useful for measuring heights of growing children as well as carpentry and building work.

21. TACK HAMMER: with tapered head (or pein) for tapping in small nails and tacks in awkward positions.

22. TENON SAW: a squat, sturdy saw for accurate cutting of timber joints.

Powerful Additions

POWER DRILL: either electrical or cordless, takes much of the hard work out of drilling. With variable speed control you can drill into materials of different densities without burning out the motor. Also purchase a selection of drill bits.

POWER SANDER: enables you to smooth out blemishes in timber and plaster in a fraction of the time it would take with sanding block and paper.

GAS, ELECTRICITY AND WATER

Once a house has been built and the services have been inspected by the relevant authorities, meters are installed to record the amount of gas, electricity and water used by the household. At the meter there is a switch or tap which enables the mains supply to be turned off. With gas and water supplies, the meters are located close to the front boundary. If you cannot find a meter or mains tap, it may be buried or concealed by dense growth. Contact your authority and ask for a plan of the service or arrange an appointment with an inspector who will locate the source of supply to your property.

Old and antiquated meters and taps are being replaced quickly. If yours falls into this category, ask for a demonstration of turning it on and off; replacements will be self explanatory and, in the case of a gas meter, the mains supply is switched off when the indent on the valve is at an angle of 90 degrees to the pipe.

To switch off the water, turn off the cock or tap which will be on the front boundary side of the water meter; check a nearby garden tap, if the mains tap is off no water will flow when the garden tap is turned on.

The electrical meter board is contained in a sturdy metal box and is generally attached to an exterior front wall of the house at adult eye-level. The service cable, carrying 240 volts of electric power, passes through the supplying authority's sealed fuse and a meter which calculates the amount of electricity used. This same cable then reaches the mains switch which enables all electricity in the house to be cut off. From the mains switch the electricity is distributed throughout the house via several circuits.

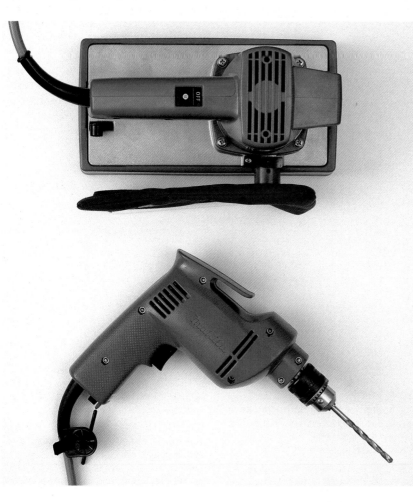

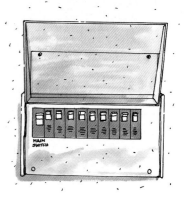

The usual plan entails separate circuits for the oven, water heater, power and lights, these are labelled accordingly on the board. Each circuit has its own safety valve, be it fuse or circuit breaker. The old system of fuse holders, containing fuse wire for each circuit, has long been superseded by circuit breakers which are safer and easier to reset than their predecessors. If you still have fuse holders, the wiring in your house is very old and is very likely unsafe; have it rewired as soon as possible with circuit breakers. Never try to alter or add to electrical circuits; these are jobs for licensed electricians.

Basic Electrical Terms

ALTERNATING CURRENT (a.c.): electricity generated for public use is in the form of a.c.

AMPERAGE (amp): unit measuring the amount of current in a circuit.

CIRCUIT: the path around which an electrical current flows.

CONDUCTOR: anything which carries an electrical current.

DIRECT CURRENT (d.c.): electric current which flows in only one direction, e.g. from a battery.

EARTH: the path along which a current flows to the ground safely. Objects which are not earthed properly cannot handle the heat generated and will melt or catch on fire.

FUSE: a connection which cuts off the current if a circuit is overloaded or a fault occurs.

LIVE: a circuit through which a current is flowing.

TRANSFORMER: a device which converts one a.c. voltage to another.

VOLT: a unit which measures the pressure that drives a current around a circuit.

WATT: a unit of power measuring the amount of electricity an appliance used.

CRACKS

TO FILL CRACKS IN A WALL
Cracks often look worse than they are. Usually they are the result of settlement or shrinkage which happens after a house has been built. Fill them and they probably won't occur again. Cracks in rendering on exterior walls are not just unsightly, they will allow moisture to penetrate to inside rooms. Tap the render around the crack; if it sounds hollow or "drummy" (as it is called in the trade) it has come away from the wall. Remove loose render with a hammer and cold chisel, and fill it with concrete render. If the mix is too wet it will fall out of the crack; have it slightly on the dry side.

If the crack is very large, a tradesman should repair it. When pointing between existing brickwork has become cracked or powdery, dig it out with a hammer and cold chisel and soak the area thoroughly with water. Then repoint with a mixture of 1 part cement, 1 part lime and 6 parts sand, filling the vertical joints before the horizontal and working from the top to the bottom.

Fill fine cracks in internal plaster walls with plaster if you have any, or one of the proprietary fillers. Surface blemishes left by nail holes in walls and woodwork should be filled with a cellulose based filler.

Larger cracks or holes in plaster walls can be packed with newspaper soaked in proprietary filler before being smoothed over with the same substance. Alternatively, pack the gap with papier mache, which is made with torn up newspapers soaked in a concentrated wallpaper paste, and finish with a filler when dry. Sand flat and paint.

Cracks may occur in plasterboard panels due to movement. Rectify with plaster instead of other fillers; plaster has a better chance of not cracking again.

DAMP

TO TEST FOR DAMP
You can usually smell damp in a room and even the best ventilated houses can suffer from damp areas, especially cupboards, after long spells of rain.

To test for damp use a piece of aluminium foil, stick it to the wall with removable tape and leave it for a day.

If moisture appears on the exposed surface of the foil, the dampness is caused by condensation. Leave the windows open and encourage cross draughts. In a kitchen, an extractor fan will draw off steam and heat.

When you examine the other side of the foil and find there are signs of moisture, the dampness is penetrating from an outside source.

Check for cracks in outside walls or problems with gutters and downpipes. After repairs to the defective areas the walls will dry out. Wait until a spell of dry weather before painting water damaged walls.

Rising damp, which comes from the ground when there is a defective or non-existent damp course, can ruin plaster, paintwork and wallpaper. The line of damp will fluctuate, rising higher up the wall in wet weather. Have a professional attend to the problem, but wait until all the structure is completely dry before replastering and decorating.

TO SILENCE A SQUEAKING DOOR
Oil hinges thoroughly and work the oil well into them. Grease is best on outdoor hinges.

TO FIX A STICKING DOOR
Paint can build up on the hinge side of the door and cause difficulties. Strip paint away and repaint.

If the door sticks on the other side (the jamb side where you open obstinate screw top bottles), first support the door with wedges before removing the door and hinges and then excavate the frame's hinge recesses with a chisel; then rehang the door. Scraping on the floor can be eliminated by placing a sheet of abrasive paper on the floor, remove the door and plane away excess timber.

TO TIGHTEN LOOSE HINGES
If the hinges wobble, support the door first with wedges before unscrewing one hinge at a time. Cut firm cardboard to size, pack into hinge recess and replace the hinge. Repeat for all hinges.

WHEN THE SCREW HOLES ARE TOO LARGE
Pack screw holes which have become enlarged with matchsticks, splinters of timber or small dowels. Some wood fillers are structurally sound when dry so you could fill the hole with wood filler and redrill the hole before inserting the screw.

TO FIX A STICKING LOCK
Sometimes locks stick when a door frame subsides or shrinks. Propping up the door may enable you to lock and unlock the door but a permanent solution would be to have the lock refitted by an expert.

For a less dramatic problem, a sticking lock may be loosened by applying lubricating oil and working the lock forcefully several times with the key. Alternatively, cover the key with graphite pencil and insert and work the key into the lock.

DOWNPIPES

TO CLEAR A DOWNPIPE

When down pipes are blocked with leaves, runoff from the roof can't drain away properly and water damage to walls could ensue. Another ill effect is that wet leaves will eventually corrode the blocked pipe.

If you can't extract the blockage from the ground end of the pipe, attack the problem from above with a long piece of timber or bamboo and push the debris into a bin at the bottom of the pipe. If the timber itself won't shift the mass, tie a stone in a rag to the end of it to give this improvised tool a little more clout.

FLOORS

TO STOP FLOOR BOARDS CREAKING

Floor boards squeak when they are loose and can be secured by hammering long floor nails into the joists through the boards. Rows of nail heads indicate the position of joists beneath the boards.

The creak may also be eradicated by blowing talcum powder, which acts as a lubricant, into the crack between the offending boards.

TO SILENCE CREAKING STAIRS

Brush dressmaker's marking chalk into the space between stair and riser or push PVA glue into the crack using a spreader made from a piece of cardboard – firstly prising open the gap with a chisel.

If you have access to the underside of the stair, a more structural solution is to brace the tread and riser joints with triangular chocks of timber or metal brackets.

FUSES

A BLOWN FUSE

If a fuse blows or a circuit-breaker trips, this is a warning that something is wrong, either with a light-globe, an appliance or appliance cord or with the wiring itself.

Switch off the mains switch and find the blown fuse by checking each fuse holder, putting each one back before taking out the next. A fused circuit-breaker will have its switch in the "off" position. Inside the house, switch off all light switches or unplug all appliances on the defective circuit, examine each one for a sign of excessive heat or smoke staining and you may locate the problem. If the fault is a cord or appliance, have it professionally repaired or replace it altogether. Reset the circuit breaker or replace the fuse wire (see instructions at right) and switch on the mains switch.

Systematically switch on each light or appliance until the full quota is operating. The fuse may blow again during this experiment and you will be able to isolate the offending appliance and have it repaired. When everything is on and the fuse blows it may be because the circuit is overloaded. If you cannot discover the problem, call an electrician.

The most up-to-date switchboards have safety switches (formally earth leakage circuit breakers) combined with circuit breakers on protected power circuits (just like an old fuse or normal circuit breaker would), in addition, they offer personal protection from active to earth faults which are the most common cause of electrocution. The majority of fatalities occur from portable appliances and extension leads and not from heavy stationary appliances such as stove, refrigerators or lights.

Sometimes an electrical fault will trip off power to the circuit. If this goes unnoticed during holidays or a day-long absence and the refrigerator or freezer is on a protected circuit, food may spoil before the fault is rectified. It is for this reason that safety switches are put on circuits where the risk is greatest, and not where they may cause food loss. Safety switches are such a good idea, most electricity authorities are going to make them compulsory in every new home.

For individual circuit protection in existing installations, have a safety switch double power point installed; it will replace a standard power point. When it is first on the circuit, it protects all other standard power points "downstream".

Then there are safety switch extension cords, safety switches which plug into standard power points and safety switch powerboards with four or six outlets; these devices give personal protection against electrocution by switching off the power as soon as an imbalance of power is detected. Of course safety switches are no substitute for commonsense, and all the usual precautions should be taken when using electrically powered tools and appliances.

TO REPAIR A FUSE

With any kind of electrical repair or investigation, always remember to turn off the mains switch at the meter box first.

Inspect each fuse, replacing each one in turn until you find one with its wire strip melted.

Loosen screws and remove both pieces of the old wire and clean away any scorching.

Replace with a new wire of correct thickness and length, screwed between the terminals; start by winding around the shaft of one screw clockwise, tighten the screw, thread the wire to the other screw, finish with a clockwise twist and tighten this screw. Replace fuse, switch on mains switch.

Refer to A Blown Fuse (left) to isolate the cause of the problem.

TO CLEAN GUTTERS

If you have to use a ladder to reach the gutter, make sure the ladder is sound and that it is placed evenly on the ground. You should never step beyond the third last rung of the ladder.

Scrape leaves out of the gutter with a trowel and put them in the compost heap.

If you don't like heights, you could use a garden vacuum cleaner for the job. Some models come with a special hook attachment and you use the blowing action to blow leaves out. It is best to wear goggles and place protective plastic mesh over down pipe holes to prevent leaves being forced into drains.

HEATERS

TO CLEAN A HEATER

Any kind of heater, whether it is built in, portable or just a discreet grille in the wall or floor, needs little more than regular dusting.

Static dusters, twirled vigorously between your hands before using, actively attract dust. These are particularly good for cleaning grilles on wall-unit gas and electric heaters.

If a heater has been unused for some time and you want to avoid that first blast of dust when you switch on the fan, carefully go over the grille with a vacuum cleaner. Make sure the heater is switched off before you clean it.

TO CHANGE A LIGHTBULB

When the bulb in a table or standard lamp blows, switch off at the lamp, switch off at the wall and unplug the cord. Wait for the bulb to cool down before removing it with your hand enclosed in a tea towel.

If the light takes a bayonet bulb, you will have to push against it slightly and turn it clockwise to release the pins from the socket. Replace with a new bulb, pushing firmly but gently into the socket and turning it anti-clockwise.

A screw-in bulb screws out anti-clockwise and screws in clockwise.

Plug in cord, switch on at the wall and switch on the lamp.

When removing a light-globe from a ceiling fitting, switch it off at the switch first before removing it.

TO REMOVE
A BROKEN LIGHTBULB

With a standard or table lamp, switch off at lamp, then at the wall and unplug cord. Use needle-nosed pliers to get a grip on the metal sleeve of the bulb which goes into the socket. Twist in the correct manner for the type of bulb. If the bulb is stuck firmly, take the lamp to a lighting shop.

When a bulb breaks in a ceiling fitting, switch off the power at the mains switch and remove relevant fuse cartridge or switch off the circuit-breaker.

Wearing gloves and goggles, try to loosen the remains of the bulb with needle-nosed pliers twisting according to the type of bulb. If you cannot free the bulb, call in an electrician.

TO CHANGE
A QUARTZ HALOGEN BULB

NEVER touch a quartz halogen globe with your fingers. They are very sensitive and the heat and pressure of your fingertip could ruin a good globe instantly. Always use a paper facial tissue when picking up one of these delicate bulbs.

Some of the dichroic lamps which take halogen bulbs require nothing other than gentle pressure to slip the bulb into the socket. Others have holders which have to be unscrewed first, then the bulb is inserted and the screws replaced. Others still have springs which hold the bulb in and some models are very complicated and need individual explanation.

The best plan is to ask your low-voltage lighting retailer at the time of purchase to give you a personal demonstration on how to replace a bulb. Also, buy some replacement bulbs when you buy your lamp because your corner store won't have them.

TO FIX A LEAKING PIPE TEMPORARILY

Dripping pipes signal cracking or corrosion and should be replaced with copper pipes which are trouble free. However, old galvanised iron pipes can be temporarily repaired.

Start by turning off the water supply at the mains, including the hot water system, drain the pipes by turning on all the taps.

For a small leak, dry the surface of pipe before wrapping it with plumber's waterproof tape, or simply rub the leak with petroleum jelly and bind the pipe tightly with rag. Alternatively, bind the pipe with waterproof tape.

Make the repair more permanent with one of the "miracle" adhesives or putties in conjunction with fibreglass or plumber's tape. Take notice of the drying time – a whole day is probably too long to wait. Choose a preparation with a shorter drying time.

Roughen the surface of the pipe first with fine rasp, file or glass paper. Following manufacturer's instructions, combine resin and hardener and apply to leak.

Wrap the ruptured area with tape and apply more of the adhesive or putty mix.

Leave to set hard before turning on mains tap. To prevent an airlock forming, leave all taps open until water flows.

TO THAW A FROZEN PIPE

Do not use a blowtorch to thaw a pipe; it is too easy to start a fire. Instead try an electric hot-air paint stripper on the frozen pipe.

If you don't have a paint stripper, a hair dryer will work, but it will be a much slower process.

Unthaw the pipe slowly, the ice may already have cracked the pipe and you could end up with an instant flood! If the pipe has obviously burst, turn off the water at the mains before attempting any thawing.

If you don't have a hair dryer, apply a hot water bottle or hot cloths along the pipe little by little until the water begins to flow again.

PLUGS

TO WIRE A PLUG

Wiring a plug is a professional's job but some manufacturers do include diagrams and instructions on the packaging of their products. The majority of domestic accidents involving electricity occur because of wrongly connected plugs and sockets, and damaged and worn cords. If the earth wire is not connected to the earth terminal, death could ensue through electrocution. Discarded old electrical cords and plugs. Modern plugs are much safer than old models; never fit a new cord with an old plug. Buy new, ready-made extension cords; have one with a safety switch for portable tools such as the power drill or appliances you use outdoors (eg. an electric barbecue).

Connecting the right wires to the right terminals is vitally important when wiring a plug.

IN RECENT FLEXES

1 Connect green-and-yellow wires to Earth **marked E**

2 Connect blue wires to Neutral **marked N**

3 Connect brown wires to Active **marked A**

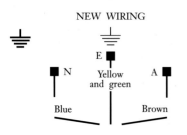

NEW WIRING

E
N   Yellow   A
     and green
Blue   Brown

OLD WIRING

E
N   Green   A
Black   Red

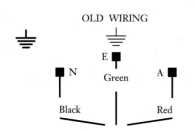

IN OLD FLEXES

1 Connect green wires to Earth **marked E**

2 Connect black wires to Neutral **marked N**

3 Connect red wires to Active **marked A**

New plugs with a push-fit action are the easiest to wire.

Separate the three components of the plug; the clamp which holds the flex in place, the cover and plug workings.

Thread the flex through the clamp and cover. Using wire strippers and being careful not to cut into the insulation of the wires, cut away 50mm (or the length recommended) of the outer sheathing of the flex. Then put the wires approximately in place on the back of the plug.

Strip away 6mm (or the length recommended) of the coloured insulation with wire strippers; this exposed wire goes around the terminal screws.

Twist these exposed wires clockwise (no straggly ends now!), referring once again to the connecting wire chart, set the wire twists in place and screw them down securely. Clip the cover over the plug and screw clamp down to hold the flex in place.

SINKS

TO CLEAR A BLOCKED SINK

Clear the sink of its contents leaving a little water over the plug hole and use a plunger to shift the blockage. Put the rubber cup of the plunger over the outlet and pump plunger repeatedly. In a bathroom, block the sink overflow with your hand, some rag or tape in order to create the required vacuum which will dislodge the blockage material. Also cover extra plugholes in a double or triple kitchen sink.

If the sink is still blocked, place a bucket under the pipes before undoing the nut at the U bend and searching for the blockage through the hole with a length of wire bent into a hook. Pull the blocked material into the bucket and replace the nut. Pour a cup of washing soda crystals down the sink and flush it through with a kettle full of boiling water.

Never use caustic soda in a blocked sink. If grease is present, a hard soap-like substance will form and block the drain further. If you then can't find the blockage, don't be tempted to persist, call a plumber.

TO PREVENT
SINK BLOCKAGES

✏ After frying food, drain off melted fat, allow it to harden, scrape the hardened fat onto newspaper and put in the bin.

✏ Don't pour melted or congealed fat down the drain.

✏ Never put disposable nappies down the toilet.

✏ Kitchen paper and tissues should go in the bin, not in the drainage or sewer system.

✏ Hair is a classic cause of blockages – clear it away from the floor waste in the shower and put it in the bin; don't flush it down the toilet.

✏ Put coffee grounds and tea leaves in the compost heap or bin – not down the sink.

✏ Flush out the waste disposal unit at least once a week.

✏ Use a rubber or plastic spatula to remove oil and grease from pans then fill them, prior to washing, with hot water and a squirt of dish-washing liquid to break up fat particles.

✏ You can help prevent blockages in drains and sinks without using earth-harming chemicals. A cup of washing soda, vinegar or a combination of salt and bicarbonate of soda followed by a kettle full of hot water, will scour and freshen drains; perform this cleaning process once a week.

TAP WASHERS

TO REPLACE A TAP WASHER

Conventional taps have washers which eventually become worn away by turning them on and off, and dripping ensues.

The more expensive ceramic disc taps are washerless, if they start to drip the problem will need expert attention; call a plumber.

Washers come in different sizes; buy a selection if you don't know the right size for your tap.

Turn off water supply at the mains. Turn on tap until water stops running. Plug sink.

To unscrew the head from the body, use a wrench with a piece of soft rag protecting the tap from the tool. To stop the whole tap from turning, secure the bottom with another wrench and piece of rag.

Tap models vary and some have a retaining screw on the handle or capstan head which must be loosened first in order to gain access to the adaptor nut which is unscrewed to remove the tap head. This retaining screw could be on the side of the handle or under a colour-coded screw or snap-down button. If your tap has a plastic surround, lever this off carefully.

Unscrew the tap head and remove the valve which contains the washer.

Take off the old washer by holding the valve with pliers and unscrewing the nut with a spanner.

Fit new washer, reassemble tap, remove plug and turn on water supply. Leave tap on until water starts to flow to prevent an airlock in the pipes.

TOILET

TO FIX A BLOCKED TOILET

A blocked toilet is a serious health hazard and a licensed plumber should be called immediately. Don't flush the toilet or the pan will overflow. Pumping with a toilet plunger by moving it up and down forcefully in the neck of the bowl may shift the blocked material. If you don't have a toilet plunger, you could improvise with a sturdy, wooden-handled toilet brush (not a fragile plastic handled model) and tie an old towel over the brush.

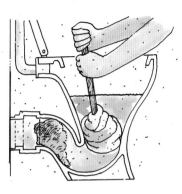

Before attempting any home repairs to plumbing and sewerage systems, check your local building and health regulations first. Prevention is preferable to repair, see list of tips under Preventing Sink Blockages, page 98.

TO FIX AN OVERFLOWING CISTERN

Remove the lid from the cistern, you may have to unscrew the plunger button on top.

By raising the lever arm with your fingers you can immediately stop the overflow; in a raised position, the arm closes off the inlet valve. Support the arm in the raised position with a ruler or coat hanger across the top of the cistern. Attach the arm to the support with a twist tie or string.

The ball float may be damaged and need replacing. Unscrew the old one and fit a new ball float to the arm.

Alternatively, the supporting float arm may be angled incorrectly which would interfere with the shutting off of the inlet valve. With a metal arm, use a spanner to bend the float end down so the float sits lower in the water. With a plastic float arm, lower the float by loosening the nut on the arm.

The washer on the inlet valve may need replacing. When worn, the valve could drip constantly and finally flood the cistern. Turn off the water supply to the cistern, remove the device which connects the arm and valve (usually a split pin) and remove the washer. Replace it with a new one, connect the arm and valve again and replace the lid on the cistern.

TO CLEAN A WASTE DISPOSAL UNIT

With the unit on, run cold water into the sink and add a slice of lemon to make it smell fresh. There is no need to use harsh chemicals to clean the unit when a lemon slice and water are quite satisfactory. Harsh chemicals may even damage the unit.

If the unit becomes clogged, most modern models have a freeing mechanism. If there is no such mechanism, switch off the power to the machine at the mains. Through the sink outlet, connect the release tool for your unit onto the nut on the blades and jiggle the tool until the motor is free. Remove the tool, turn on the power at the mains and then turn on the cold tap and switch on the unit.

To prevent blockages in a waste disposal unit, NEVER put these items into the unit: boxes, china, cotton wool, cutlery, fat (hot or cold), glass, large bones, metals, plastic, cloths, onion skins or string.

TO REPAIR A CRACKED WINDOW

If the window is only cracked you may be able to apply waterproof tape to the crack. Before attempting this, put on heavy leather gloves and wear strong, covered-in shoes and goggles or sunglasses to protect your eyes.

For extra support, ask an adult to hold a flat object such as a breadboard in a bath towel, with the ends of the towel bunched into a "handle" against the crack from the other side of the window. Tape the crack from both sides, supporting the crack again with the breadboard in the towel.

If the tape method won't hold, remove the glass and cover the gap temporarily with heavy clear plastic sheeting, tacked into position. To remove glass, crisscross the broken window with masking tape, hold a cloth against the top of the glass with one hand and with the other, hammer through the cloth to break up the glass. Work from the top to the bottom to reduce chance of injury from flying glass. Remove all glass carefully, wrap it in many sheets of newspaper before disposing of it.

TO REPLACE A WINDOW PANE

Wearing heavy gloves, covered-in shoes and goggles or sunglasses, remove broken glass, (see method in To Repair a Cracked Window, above).

Scrape out old putty with screwdriver and use pliers and the handle of a hammer to remove any other fragments of glass.

Pull out glazing pins with pincers and smooth and clean out the window recess using glass paper if necessary.

Measure the opening carefully and have the glass cut 1.5 mm smaller than the opening on all four sides to allow for expansion.

Brush away sawdust and residue and paint recess with primer. Allow to dry before applying putty.

Brush the glass recess with linseed oil before pressing in moulded putty. This is the seal which is inside the room. Pick up the glass pane and press it firmly into position around the edges, but not in the centre. The putty will hold the pane in place while you tap in the glazing pins.

Gently tap glazing pins into the recess using the side of a broad chisel as a hammer. This is a delicate operation; slide the chisel along the glass to lessen the impact. In old fashioned, metal framed windows, special clips are pressed into the sash and these take the place of glazing pins.

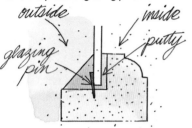

With a putty knife, spread putty around the edge of the pane using adjacent windows as a guide to the depth and angle. Mitre the putty at each corner for a neat finish.

Trim away excess putty with a putty knife, remove fingerprints with window cleaner and leave for at least a week before applying paint. Don't leave the putty unpainted for too long or the surface will start to break down.

TO FREE A STICKING WINDOW

Shrinkage in timber may cause loosened joints and result in a sticking window. Fortunately, four metal brackets can solve the problem. With the window closed, push the window back into shape by driving timber wedges between the window and the frame; the window is "true" when the gaps in the joints are closed.

Fit bracket over one corner joint of the window, mark screw positions with a bradawl then fix bracket.

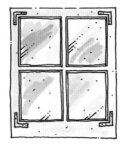

Secure the other three corners of the window in the same way; remove wedges.

TO FIX A RATTLING WINDOW

The simplest way to take the rattle out of a window is to fit an insulating strip between the window and its frame.

If the rattle is caused by loose or missing putty, reputty the recess, see To Replace a Window Pane, page 99.

CHOOSING TRADESPEOPLE

Although much in the way of maintenance and repairs can be done by the householder, there are times when the experts have to be called in. This is especially true in the case of problems with electrical appliances and wiring, plumbing and drainage, and gas appliances where strict regulations apply.

For large jobs you should obtain at least three quotes from three separate tradespeople. Personal recommendations from friends or neighbours give most householders a feeling of security. Failing this, you may be able to find tradesmen on building, renovation or extension sites in your neighbourhood.

For small jobs, most people phone the tradesperson who did some major project on their house. Notice boards in shopping centres, local papers and the Yellow Pages will reveal names and you can then ask the tradespeople you contact for recent references.

Once you've found a good tradesperson, take a little time to watch him/her at work; there is plenty to learn about quick, easy and efficient ways of effecting a repair.

If you have a specific plumbing problem, you may be able to entice a plumber to your house if there is a half day or a day's work involved. Think of other small repairs which need to be done and you may finish up getting four small jobs done for the same price as it may have cost you to fix a leak.

PAINTING

No doubt there will come a time when that painting job just has to be done, whether it be simple touch-up to the skirting boards or repainting the entire house. Be organised, you'll be surprised how much easier the task will be. The information on the following will help you to be prepared.

Dulux

CHOOSING PAINT

Decide on the type of paint you want before you decide on the colour; the finish you require may not be available in every colour. Here are some basic guidelines:

OIL-BASED PAINTS: are the hardest wearing and offer good coverage. Available in flat, semi-gloss and full-gloss finishes, these enamel paints are thinned with turpentine or paint thinners and need lots of time to dry between coats. Oil-based paints are recommended for interior woodwork which sees a lot of wear, and are good for utility areas such as the kitchen, bathroom and laundry.

Full-gloss will take the most punishment but will show up surface irregularities.

PLASTIC PAINTS: are fast-drying, can be thinned with water and painting equipment can be washed out in water. Generally, those made of 100 percent acrylic are considerd the best. These paints have less of a "paint smell" and are available in flat, gloss, low-sheen and satin finishes. Plastic paints are favoured for walls and ceilings in bedroom and living areas.

POLYURETHANES: are more popular than varnishes these days. They are used to seal timber surfaces which get a lot of wear - floors and benchtops. Polyurethanes require turpentine or paint thinners for cleaning up.

NON-DRIP PAINTS: are available in enamel and plastic. It is particularly good for ceilings because it will not run or sag. Some non-drip paints are almost solid in form.

Equipment

How much equipment you buy will depend on how much painting you have to do. Opt for good quality tools, they last longer and give a better finish. Buy brushes with natural, rather than synthetic, bristles as the bristles don't fall out as easily. Remember too, if you look after your equipment it will last for years.

Basic set of brushes
Bucket
Drop sheet or newspaper
Extension handle for roller
Filling knife
Masking tape
Mineral turpentine
Putty knife
Roller and roller sleeves
Roller tray
Rubber gloves
Sandpaper
Scraping knife

BEFORE YOU START

✆ Remove as much furniture as possible, push the rest to the centre of the room and cover it.

✆ Remove pictures, light fittings, window fittings and door handles. Mask off light and power switches with masking tape, remove the surrounds if possible.

✆ Cover the floor with newspaper, old sheets or a plastic drop cloth.

✆ Every surface that is to be painted must be clean, dry and smooth. Wash down the walls with sugar soap or a special paint cleanser. Remove all traces of mould and mildew with a solution of household bleach.

✆ Walls that have been painted with distemper or Kalsomine (this frequently occurs in old houses) must be thoroughly washed and coated with a binder before you paint on a new colour. To check if distemper has been used, wet your fingers and press them against the surface, if they come away powdery it is distemper. New paint will peel off if painted over distemper.

✎ Clean out any chips or dents, fill with a wall filler, smooth over with your finger or a knife, sand it level before sealing and painting. Large areas should be done in two or three stages to allow it to dry in between applications. See Cracks at beginning of this chapter.

✎ DO NOT use a blowtorch on plaster walls, asbestos sheeting, around glass or on softwood boards as you will start a fire.

✎ NEVER use a blowtorch on old paint. It may contain lead and give off poisonous fumes.

✎ If using a chemical stripper, wear old gloves, goggles and protective clothing.

✎ DO NOT smoke if using a chemical stripper; they are highly flammable.

PAINT QUANTITIES

✎ Details of the coverage you can expect are given on most tins – use this as a guide but remember, the spread of the paint depends on the texture and condition of the surface, the quality of the brushes, rollers and the weather.

✎ Paint quantities can be calculated in this way. Multiply the ceiling height by the combined length of the four walls, then deduct for the large areas not being painted (windows and doors). A room that is four metres long by three metres wide with a ceiling height of three metres will have a paint area of 42 square metres. That's 4 + 4 + 3 + 3 = 14 metres x 3 = 42 square metres, minus doors and windows. The ceiling area is 3 metres x 4 metres = 12 square metres.

Figures for coverage will be for one coat, mostly you'll need two coats at least for a good job. Small amounts of left-over paint can be used for maintenance touch-ups!

SURFACES

PAINTING OVER WALLPAPER: there are some wallpapers that are designed to be painted over; they are used when walls are in bad condition. They have a thick textured surface and a range of patterns. Generally, however, wallpaper should be removed before painting. You can hire a wallpaper steamer to do this. If you intend to paint over the paper, test a small hidden area with the paint to check that the pattern does not bleed through the paint, and does not bubble.

PREVIOUSLY-PAINTED SURFACES: plastic paint should be used over plastic paint and oil-based over oil-based. Remember this when buying your undercoat! If you don't know what has been used previously, wet a wad of paper towelling and tape it to the wall. Leave overnight and remove following morning. If the paint has shrivelled it is probably plastic, if not it's probably oil-based.

Gloss paint should be lightly sanded to remove any loose or flaking paint. If you are not sure if the old paintwork is suitable to paint over, place a strip of adhesive tape on the wall and pull it off quickly. If the paint comes off, you will have to take the lot off, otherwise you risk the paint peeling away when you add the new coat.

Strip the paint with a stripping knife, shave hook or chemical stripper, wash the surface and seal before applying the new paint.

UNPAINTED SURFACES: plaster or cement should be completely dry and any imperfections repaired. If you are using an oil-based top coat, apply a coat of sealer, then an oil-based undercoat. Plaster or plastic paint does not need a sealer.

VARNISHED TIMBER: sand lightly, seal to prevent stain bleeding through the new paintwork.

WINDOWS: mask inside frames with masking tape. Remove tape before paint is completely dry to stop tape pulling paint off.

PAINTING TECHNIQUES

✎ Stir the paint thoroughly so the colour is evenly mixed. Using a flat stick, move the paint up and down in a scooping motion. Storing the paint upside down before you are ready to use it will stop the pigment settling on the bottom.

✎ For best results work in this sequence: ceilings, walls, windows, doors, skirting boards, cabinets, cupboards and shelves.

✎ Brushes and rollers will hold more paint if they are dampened first with the appropriate thinner, then rolled or brushed out on a towel until quite dry. This makes the clean-up easier too.

✎ Always sand and paint woodwork in the direction of the grain; never in circles.

✎ Set aside at least four uninterrupted hours so that you are working in the same light and you can finish at least one coat.

✎ If using a roller, paint the corner of the room where the ceiling meets the walls with a narrow brush; the roller will not reach these areas.

✎ Use a roller with a long pile for textured surfaces.

✎ If using plastic paint and a brush, apply even strokes about half a metre long, then paint over the area, switching the direction of the strokes. Brush INTO the wet paint.

✎ If using oil-based paint and a brush, paint a strip about half a metre square, brush carefully in one direction, then again at right angles.

✎ If using a roller, the paint should cover about three-quarters of the bottom of the tray. Work the roller up and down the tray to make sure the paint is evenly distributed. Make broad sweeps with the roller, but don't roll too fast. Make sure the roller cover fits the roller neatly; this will prevent "tracks".

CARE OF PAINTING EQUIPMENT

✎ If you use water-based paint, wash the brushes in water and detergent after you finish painting.

✎ If you use oil-based paint or polyurethanes, clean the brushes in mineral turpentine, then wash them with soap and water.

✎ Dry the brushes with the bristles held together with a rubber band.

Before washing rollers, roll them out on newspaper to remove excess paint.

✎ Clean with soap and water if water-based paint has been used.

✎ It's a good idea to have spare roller sleeves if you are using gloss paint. Cleaning takes a long time and is quite messy.

✎ Keep leftover paint in an air-tight container small enough to be almost filled. Seal all tins tightly and to prevent a skin forming, store tins upside down. Store flammable paints in a safe place, well away from children.

WALLPAPERING

Preparation is the key to successful wallpapering. Your walls should be prepared in the same way as when you are painting – wash, patch, remove flaking paint and seal all the surfaces before you begin unrolled paper and pasting it.

Equipment

Broad knife

Bucket

Large table

Measuring tape

Paste brush

Pencil

Plumb line

Scissors

Seam roller

Smoothing brush

Sponge

Stanley knife

Trough for ready-pasted paper

BEFORE YOU START

☞ Remove distemper or Kalsomine (found in old houses) by washing thoroughly, then seal wall with a binder. Leave at least 72 hours before papering.

☞ Apply an anti-mould solution to cement rendered walls before sealing, and to bathroom, kitchen or laundry walls, where a reaction between wallpaper paste and damp could encourage mould to grow. Non-porous vinyls and foils also require anti-mould treatment.

☞ As with painting, move all furniture to the centre of the room and cover it, cover the floor with newspaper, old sheets or a plastic drop sheet.

Remove all light fittings, switch and power point covers.

REMOVING OLD WALLPAPER

☞ Old wallpaper should be removed where possible with warm water, a wallpaper stripping solution or a hired wallpaper steamer.

☞ If stripping wallpaper by hand, soak the paper with warm water using a cloth or sponge. If the paper is old and refuses to come off the surface you may have to add a wallpaper stripper to the water.

LENGTH

METRIC	IMPERIAL
5mm	1/4in
1cm	1/2in
2.5cm	1in
5cm	2in
7cm	3in
10cm	4in
12cm	5in
15cm	6in
18cm	7in
20cm	8in
23cm	9in
25cm	10in
28cm	11in
30cm	12in (1ft)
60cm	24in (2ft)
91cm	36in (1 yard)
1 metre	39in
3.05m	10ft

Strip the paper using a scraper or stripping knife. Hold the knife at an angle to the wall, taking care not to dig into the plaster. If wallpaper is washable, score the surface, soak the paper and then scrape it off with a knife or scraper. If wallpaper is vinyl, lift the top layer from the backing paper at the bottom corners of each strip and peel off. Remove backing paper as for wallpaper.

Lightly sand the wall to remove all pieces of wallpaper.

☞ If the wallpaper has been painted over and you cannot remove it without causing damage to the wall, you will have to take the risk and paper over it. Seal the walls first and avoid a heavy paper which takes a long time to dry; it could lift the old papers in the process.

SIZING
Available in an ordinary and super grade, size is similar to a weak adhesive that is painted over the wall to provide a slightly slippery surface that makes wallpaper much easier to get into place, gives better adhesion and makes the paper easier to remove. Use the size recommended by the manufacturer, but ALWAYS use one unless the wallpaper directions specifically forbid it.

WALLPAPER QUANTITIES
Err on the generous side when buying paper, as rolls you buy later may not come in the same colour or dye lot. Many retailers will let you return unopened rolls.

Most wallpaper sample books have charts to help you calculate the number of rolls you need. If you buy from a specialist retailer the staff should be able to advise you. Take the measurements of your rooms with you, measure the height of the wall area and the length of each wall. As a precaution, take the measurements of your windows and doors with you too.

When you get the wallpaper home, check to make sure all the batch numbers are the same, also check for colour variation, and unroll them before you start to check for any imperfections.

LINING PAPER
If possible, hang paper horizontally to avoid seams coinciding. Don't overlap the pieces or the joins will be visible through the wallpaper. Sand back any lumps or bumps. Allow lining paper to dry for at least 24 hours before putting on top covering. Size the wall before putting on the lining and if the top covering is heavy, size the lining paper.

HANGING WALLPAPER

Walls
☞ Read the manufacturer's instructions, re-read them if something is not completely clear; there may be special procedures which you have to follow.

☞ Cut lengths of wallpaper at least 10cm longer than the height of the wall to be covered, to allow for variations and trimming. Also allow for pattern matching. In a straight match pattern, the same part of the pattern should be the same distance from the ceiling on each strip. Drop match patterns run alternately, every other drop the same distance from the ceiling. Random match patterns need no vertical matching.

☞ Begin wallpapering in an inconspicuous place as your last strip is unlikely to match up with your first.

☞ Work away from the light source so that any seam overlaps will not cast a shadow.

☞ Use a plumb line on each wall before you start to make sure the first drop, and the rest, hang straight. Crooked strips will become more noticeable as you progress and any imperfections should be adjusted at this time. Fix the line about 4cm less than the width of the paper out from the door frame or window frame where you are going to start, with the weighted end a few centimetres above floor level. When the line stops swinging, mark where it hangs and draw a straight line to the top of the wall.

✏ Pasting methods differ for specific wallpapers. Read the instructions accompanying the paper you buy. Ready-pasted papers are immersed in a trough of water and rolled around to ensure all paper is covered, while unpasted coverings have to have paste brushed on. All coverings must be left for a certain time (it will be on the instructions) so the paste has sufficient time to soak into the covering, making it supple and easier to handle. While you wait you can paste or soak the next roll.

✏ Lift covering from table, holding the top end between your thumb and forefingers and supporting it with your middle fingers. Climb ladder, line the first drop with the plumb line, allowing the lower half of the paper, still folded, to drop gently down. Allow room at the top to trim.

✏ Smooth paper into place with a large sponge or smoother, working downwards from the centre out. Unfold the lower section of the drop, smooth into place. Use a broad knife to press excess covering against the ceiling, doors, windows, cornices and skirting. If there is no skirting, press the covering well down behind carpet pile or against flooring before trimming.

Before you cut anything, check that your trimming knife is sharp.

✏ Follow the above procedures for the second drop, carefully matching the pattern and abutting the seams exactly (some coverings will require overlapped seams which can be trimmed later, this will be mentioned in the manufacturer's instructions).

✏ Check regularly for air bubbles before the paste dries out; these can be removed by rubbing gently with the smoother. Wipe seams with a dry sponge to remove any paste overlap.

Ceilings
This is a difficult job made easier with the help of another person. Work from a sturdy platform, a table (covered) or a plank between two ladders. If possible, paper across the narrowest width of the room.

✏ Mark a guideline across the ceiling, as far from the wall as the width of paper minus 25mm (trim this off when the paper is securely in place).

✏ Measure, cut and paste the paper before folding it (pasted sides together) in easy-to-handle lengths. This is where your helper comes in handy: she/he will hold the lengths as you place the paper in position on the ceiling.

✏ Place one fold at a time, smoothing it with a sponge or smoother before moving on to the next fold.

✏ Light fittings: turn the power off, remove the shade and globe. Pull the light to one side, hold the paper up close, make a hole

with scissors in the paper and pull the cord through. Make cuts around base and when the rest of the length is in position, trim and butt the paper into place around fitting.

✏ Abut other seams together, using a seam roller to secure seams.

BORDERS
These can be applied to painted or wallpapered walls once they are thoroughly dry; wait at least 48 hours after hanging wallpaper. Available both pre-pasted and unpasted, borders can be used to coordinate colours in, or add colour to a room.

✏ Use a measuring tape and straight edge to mark a guideline for your border. For horizontal borders, you can use the ceiling or floor line (whichever is closer) as a guide. If you are placing the border hard against a ceiling, measure the depth of the border plus 25mm. Use this method as a guide for the lower edge of the border, which will allow a 25mm gap for irregularities Press the border in position with a seam roller, or according to the manufacturer's instructions.

REPAIRS
Match the pattern and cut the patch to size, making it slightly larger all round. Tearing the edges of the patch gently can leave a neater and less visible joint than a straight cut line. If possible, remove the damaged section of paper before pasting the patch in place, smoothing the edges and removing any excess paste from the area.

CONSERVING ENERGY

Home insulation is an important aspect of energy saving. If we can reduce the amount of energy we use, we will reduce the emission of those gases believed responsible for over-heating the Earth's atmosphere – and cut personal costs.

Visit the Energy Information Centre in your nearest capital city, or contact your state department in charge of minerals and energy or local electricity authority. Numerous brochures and pamphlets are available on energy conservation. Write to the National Building Technology Centre, PO Box 310, North Ryde, NSW, 2113 for information on the science of building. Many of the Centre's publications deal with energy efficiency.

Solar energy systems which "harness" the sun's rays are becoming more readily available and have obvious cost benefits in the long term. Again, contact your Energy Information centre for details.

When building a house, high insulation standards must be demanded by every buyer. The Five Star Design Rating System was introduced nationwide in order to promote the building of energy-efficient homes at the lowest-possible extra cost.

Natural elements are used to their greatest advantage and local climatic conditions are taken into account when siting the house, positioning the windows and installing insulation systems. Energy Information Centres and builders can give advice on the Five Star system.

For those houses already built, conserve energy in the following ways:

✏ Check for draughts. Fix badly fitting doors and windows. Fit draught excluders to the bottom of your doors.

✏ Install thick, lined curtains in preference to double-glazing. Double glazing is better at keeping out noise than it is at keeping in heat. Draw the curtains in the evening – behind the radiators, not in front.

✏ Don't block radiators with furniture.

✏ Avoid unnecessary opening and closing of doors. Keep doors shut between heated and unheated areas of the house.

✏ Wear more clothes. It's cheaper to put on an extra sweater than it is to turn up the heater. Use more bedclothes instead of an electric blanket or take a hot-water bottle to bed. However, it is cheaper to use the electric blanket than to heat the entire bedroom with an appliance such as an electric bar heater.

✏ Inspect and maintain equipment regularly. See Household Appliances section below.

✏ Close off unused fire places.

✏ Attractive as floorboards can look, carpeting is more useful when it comes to cutting down on heat lost through the floor.

HOUSEHOLD APPLIANCES

Are your major household appliances correctly sited? Do you know how to maintain them properly? Are you using them to their maximum advantage? The following checklists will help you realise the full potential of your appliances and reduce those costly bills. Ask for advice at your local gas and electricity showrooms, and nearest Energy Information Centre.

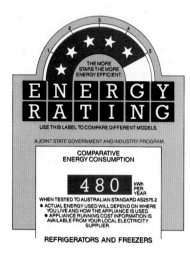

THE MORE STARS THE MORE ENERGY EFFICIENT.

ENERGY RATING

USE THIS LABEL TO COMPARE DIFFERENT MODELS.

A JOINT STATE GOVERNMENT AND INDUSTRY PROGRAM.

COMPARATIVE ENERGY CONSUMPTION

480 kWh PER YEAR

WHEN TESTED TO AUSTRALIAN STANDARD AS2575.2
● ACTUAL ENERGY USED WILL DEPEND ON WHERE YOU LIVE AND HOW THE APPLIANCE IS USED.
● APPLIANCE RUNNING COST INFORMATION IS AVAILABLE FROM YOUR LOCAL ELECTRICITY SUPPLIER.

REFRIGERATORS AND FREEZERS

THE MORE STARS THE MORE ENERGY EFFICIENT

ENERGY RATING

USE THIS LABEL TO COMPARE DIFFERENT MODELS.

A JOINT STATE GOVERNMENT AND INDUSTRY PROGRAM.

COMPARATIVE ENERGY CONSUMPTION

550

kW.h PER YEAR (USED ONCE DAILY) ON COLD WATER SUPPLY
WHEN TESTED TO AUSTRALIAN STANDARD 2007
12 PLACE SETTINGS ON ENERGYSAVE 55 PROGRAM

ACTUAL ENERGY USE AND RUNNING COST WILL DEPEND ON PROGRAM USED, WATER CONNECTION AND COST OF HOT WATER INFORMATION IS AVAILABLE FROM YOUR ENERGY SUPPLIER.

FOR HOT WATER CONNECTION
ENERGY CONSUMPTION IS **550** kW.h PER YEAR

DISHWASHER

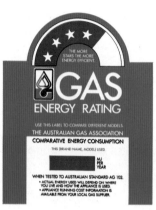

THE MORE STARS THE MORE ENERGY EFFICIENT

GAS ENERGY RATING

USE THIS LABEL TO COMPARE DIFFERENT MODELS.

THE AUSTRALIAN GAS ASSOCIATION

COMPARATIVE ENERGY CONSUMPTION

THIS (BRAND NAME, MODEL) USED

MJ PER YEAR

WHEN TESTED TO AUSTRALIAN STANDARD AG 102.
● ACTUAL ENERGY USED WILL DEPEND ON WHERE YOU LIVE AND HOW THE APPLIANCE IS USED.
● APPLIANCE RUNNING COST INFORMATION IS AVAILABLE FROM YOUR LOCAL GAS SUPPLIER.

THE MORE STARS THE MORE ENERGY EFFICIENT

ENERGY RATING

USE THIS LABEL TO COMPARE DIFFERENT MODELS.
A JOINT STATE GOVERNMENT AND INDUSTRY PROGRAM

COMPARATIVE ENERGY CONSUMPTION

COOLING
1230
kW.h PER 500 HOURS

WHEN TESTED TO AUSTRALIAN STANDARD 1861
CONDITION A THERMAL CAPACITY TYPE TEST
● ACTUAL ENERGY USED WILL DEPEND ON WHERE YOU LIVE AND HOW THE APPLIANCE IS USED.
● APPLIANCE RUNNING COST INFORMATION IS AVAILABLE FROM YOUR ELECTRICITY SUPPLIER

COOLING ONLY AIRCONDITIONER

THE MORE STARS THE MORE ENERGY EFFICIENT

COOLING HEATING

ENERGY RATING

USE THIS LABEL TO COMPARE DIFFERENT MODELS.
A JOINT STATE GOVERNMENT AND INDUSTRY PROGRAM

COMPARATIVE ENERGY CONSUMPTION

COOLING	HEATING
1020	**950**

kW.h PER 500 HOURS

WHEN TESTED TO AUSTRALIAN STANDARD 1861
CONDITION A THERMAL CAPACITY TYPE TEST
● ACTUAL ENERGY USED WILL DEPEND ON WHERE YOU LIVE AND HOW THE APPLIANCE IS USED.
● APPLIANCE RUNNING COST INFORMATION IS AVAILABLE FROM YOUR ELECTRICITY SUPPLIER

OUTPUT CAPACITY IS:-

IMPORTANT NOTE: This model is manually activated "boost" heating element will activated, reduce appliance energy efficiency and increase energy consumption.

REVERSE CYCLE AIRCONDITIONER

ENERGY RATINGS

When you are buying a new electrical appliance such as a dishwasher, fridge, freezer or air-conditioner, or a new gas appliance, look for the Energy Rating label. This supplies valuable information on the running costs inherent in each appliance, and allows you to compare the efficiency of same-sized models made by different manufacturers. The lower the energy-consumption figure, and the greater the number of stars featured on the label, the more you save on running costs. If there is no label on the appliance, ask your dealer for comparative information and evaluate the pros and cons carefully before buying.

CLOTHES DRYERS

✎ Dry full loads, not odd bits and pieces.

✎ Don't place clothes that are soaking wet into the dryer. Don't overload. Both practises mean an increase in drying time and waste of energy. Don't overdry clothes, for the same reason.

✎ Wipe out the dryer and clean the lint filter after use. Leave the door open to allow moisture to evaporate.

✎ Locate the dryer where it is exposed to fresh, dry air. If humid air is circulated through the machine, the drying time will increase.

✎ Do you really need a dryer? Drying your clothes outdoors is cheaper and cuts down on wear and tear.

DISHWASHERS

✎ Read the manufacturer's manual carefully. Load the machine as suggested.

✎ Like a car, a dishwasher needs maintenance. Clean the filter regularly to prevent clogging.

✎ "Little and often" equals "money and energy loss". Run the dishwasher when you have a full load. Washing a few items is better done by hand – it's quicker and cheaper.

✎ Use the brand of detergent recommended by the manufacturer – another brand may reduce the machine's efficiency. Measure out the exact amount specified. Try using washing soda in place of branded detergents – environmentally, it is far more friendly.

Save energy by opening the door after the rinse cycle and letting the dishes dry naturally.

When purchasing a new machine, check the Energy Rating label (see opposite page). For dishwashers, the label has two energy consumption figures because some models use hot water, some cold and some both. It is advisable to buy a dishwasher that can be connected to cold water; this allows full use of programs with various temperature settings, and also means that the machine is only heating water when required. Most of the energy used by a dishwasher is for water-heating. However, if you have an off-peak electric or high-efficiency gas hot-water system that is large enough to cope with all your household needs in addition to machine dishwashing, it can prove economical to buy a machine that connects to hot water. Connecting the appliance to hot water actually reduces the amount of time needed to complete a dishwasher cycle.

Opt for the economy or fast-wash program on your machine whenever possible.

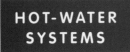

HOT-WATER SYSTEMS

Continuous electric heating is more expensive than gas or off-peak electric heating. Find out if your existing system can be converted to off-peak.

Hot-water pipes should be insulated to minimize heat loss.

Hot-water tanks should be as close as possible to the kitchen sink, where small quantities of hot water are most frequently used.

Solar systems, oil, solid-fuel, electricity and gas all have their advantages and disadvantages. Research the different systems carefully before deciding on the ideal one for your family's requirements, your pocket and your style of home.

Repair leaky hot water taps and pipes promptly.

LIGHTING

Turn off lights when not required. Leaving outdoor lights on all night is an expensive waste of energy.

Avoid using globes with a higher wattage than necessary.

Keep bulbs, reflectors and lampshades dust-free.

Fittings which hold several bulbs are usually less efficient than those that feature in a single bulb. For example, six 25W globes are required to provide the equivalent light of a 100W globe.

A lampshade made of dark, tinted glass may look attractive, but it masks the efficien-

cy of the bulb it encompasses.

Dimmer switches add flexibility to your lighting system, but do not necessarily cut energy consumption by a commensurate level: when an incandescent lamp is dimmed to a quarter its normal output, it still uses half the normal energy.

Compact fluorescent lamps are highly efficient, although a little more expensive: they use less energy and last considerably longer than traditional incandescent bulbs. Some general light fittings are able to hold a compact fluorescent lamp.

OVENS AND COOK TOPS

Coil hot-plates are considered the most energy-efficient.

Fan-forced ovens generally allow items to be cooked successfully at 20 to 30 degrees Celsius lower than conventional ovens, thereby saving costs.

A pan should always be of sufficient diameter to cover the hot-plate – energy is wasted if the pan is too small.

When food has reached the correct cooking temperature in a saucepan, put the lid on to retain the heat and turn down the power.

When baking, open the open door only when necessary and then for as short a time as possible.

Use flat-bottomed pans that cover the entire hotplate.

Microwave ovens have much to recommend them. They represent a quick and efficient use of energy. They can result in energy savings of up to 75 percent over conventional cooking methods. Microwave ovens also maintain a cooler kitchen.

REFRIGERATORS AND FREEZERS

Don't buy a model bigger than you need. Refrigerators and freezers ideally need to be three-quarters full to operate efficiently.

Upright and chest-model freezers are available in Australia. The chest model is more energy-efficient, cheaper to run and often, cheaper to buy. Check the Energy Rating label (see opposite page) before making your purchase.

Read the instruction manual to make sure you have set the temperature dial correctly. Dials can sometimes be confusing and you could find that you are increasing the temperature instead of reducing it. Refrigerators are usually set at around 4 degrees Celsius, freezers at -18 degrees Celsius. Settings that are too cold only serve

to waste energy.

Maintain a constant temperature inside your appliance. Don't open the door unnecessarily; the temperature will rise and energy will be lost.

Cool food quickly to avoid bacterial growth; then put it into the fridge or freezer. Placing hot items into the appliance will cause frost build-up and reduce the unit's efficiency.

Unless you have a frost-free model, your refrigerator must be defrosted regularly. Once ice has collected on the evaporator to a thickness of 6mm, it needs to be removed.

Check that the door grips properly – insert a piece of paper and see if it is held firmly in place. Worn seals can be replaced cheaply and avoid energy loss.

Don't place uncovered liquids in the refrigerator; they give off moisture which, in turn, increases frost build-up – frost wastes energy.

Don't place a freezer or refrigerator near a heat source such as the oven or an uninsulated wall facing the sun.

The exposed condenser coils at the back of the refrigerator should be clear of the wall by at least 8cm. Keep clean of fluff and dust.

If you are going on a holiday, or will be away for a long period, empty and clean the refrigerator and leave the door open. If you are away for a short time, leave few perishables in the appliance and adjust the dial to a warmer temperature.

Never overfill your refrigerator or freezer.

WASHING MACHINES

Don't buy a model larger than you need. If you want a top-loading model, check that it has a variable water-level facility. This allows you to cut down on water and energy consumption on those occasions when you only partly fill the machine with washing.

Unless you're in a hurry for a particular item of clothing, try to wait until you have a full load before running your machine. You'll save on energy consumption and bills.

Don't use the hot wash unless absolutely necessary. Most of the energy used in a washing machine goes on water heating. Do all rinsing, if not the entire wash, in cold water.

Do not overload your machine.

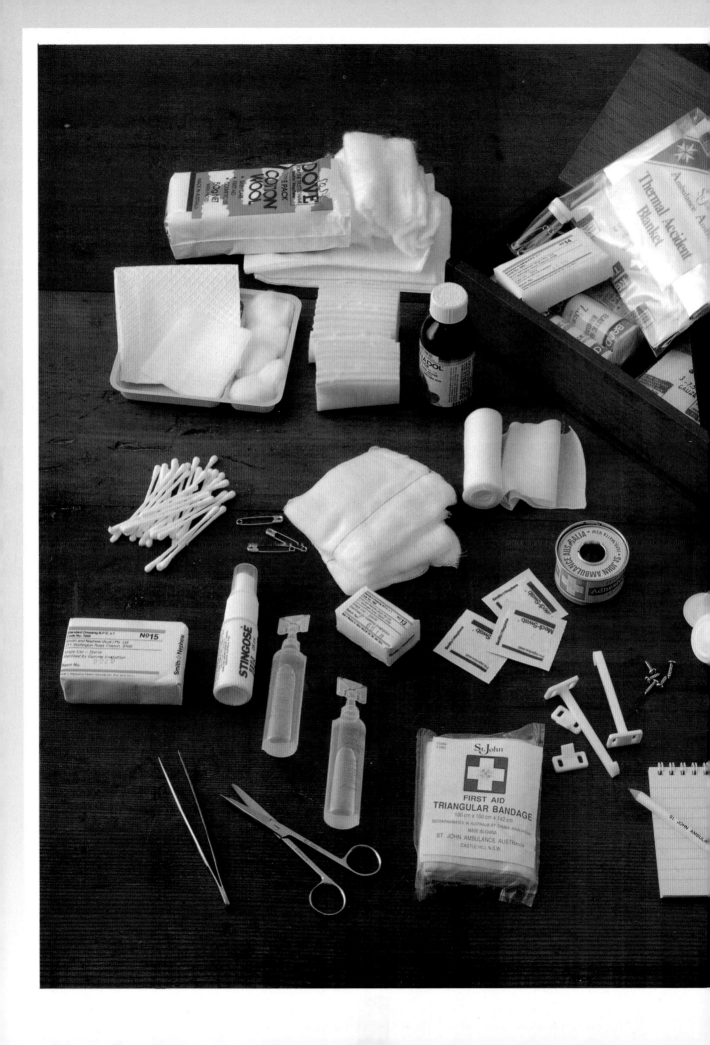

FIRST AID & SAFETY

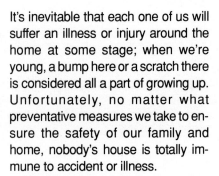

It's inevitable that each one of us will suffer an illness or injury around the home at some stage; when we're young, a bump here or a scratch there is considered all a part of growing up. Unfortunately, no matter what preventative measures we take to ensure the safety of our family and home, nobody's house is totally immune to accident or illness.

In this chapter we point out a number of safety rules, procedures, and practices that could help you avoid nasty accidents in your home. We show you how to put together a basic household first aid kit, making use of supplies from chemists as well as everyday household items.

Most importantly, we have enlisted the help of St John Ambulance to compile information – in easy-to-follow guidelines – on how to recognise and treat the common and not so common accidents that could occur around the house.

We have covered a variety of first aid situations, ranging from basic directions on how to remove an annoying splinter, through to essential resuscitation techniques.

Many mishaps that are likely to occur can easily.be prevented if all family members are made aware of and practise commonsense safety. The following instructions will help you to create a safe home environment in which your whole family can live, work and play. Take time to look around your home. Are there any items that are stored in unsafe places? Do you or your family have any bad habits that could lead to an accident? If so, act now.

INDOOR SAFETY

☞ All firearms, dangerous weapons, poisonous substances and medicines should be stored out of the reach of children. Store all dangerous items in cupboards or drawers with child-resistant locks or safety latches. Most medicines are quite safe when taken in prescribed amounts, but can easily poison young children when taken without adult supervision.

☞ Never keep old or unused medicines.

☞ Check electrical goods regularly for signs of wear. If they appear faulty, have them serviced.

☞ NEVER use or store electrical equipment in wet areas.

☞ ALWAYS use a guard for fireplaces and heaters.

☞ Sweep up broken glass immediately and wrap it well in newspaper before putting into a garbage bin.

☞ If you have glass doors or large windows around your home, make sure you mark them clearly at the eye level of all family members, using tape or felt tip pen.

Bathroom

☞ Children should always be supervised in the bathroom. It is a good idea to take the phone off the hook if bathing a child.

☞ Plugs should be out of children's reach.

☞ Store all medicines, cosmetics and razors in a medicine cabinet with a safety latch or child-resistant lock.

☞ A thermostatic mixing valve or safety tap will prevent scalds from hot water.

Kitchen

☞ Standing ovens should be bolted to the floor so they cannot be pulled over.

☞ When cooking on the stove, make sure saucepan handles face away from the front edge of the stove.

☞ Appliances should be kept well out of a child's reach. Make sure they have short cords that cannot be pulled by a child.

Laundry

☞ Store cleaning agents out of child's reach or in a cupboard with a safety latch or child-resistant lock.

☞ Store buckets (when in use), especially nappy buckets, out of child's reach to prevent drowning.

Living Areas

☞ Remove small items such as coins, batteries and jewellery from all living areas to avoid children swallowing them and choking.

☞ Cover sharp edges on tables and furniture.

☞ Loop blind and curtain cords out of children's reach to avoid the possibility of strangulation.

☞ Placemats should be used at meal times when children are at the table – a child can pull a tablecloth and scald him/herself with hot food and drink.

☞ Glass doors and large windows around the home should have safety glass or shatter-resistant film to prevent shattering if a child falls into them.

☞ Cover power points with safety plugs when not in use.

OUTDOOR SAFETY

☞ Enclose all backyard pools with a fence incorporating a child-resistant, self-closing and self-locking gate. If you have a swimming pool it is a good idea to regularly update your first aid and resuscitation skills. One of the most common causes of accidental death amongst small children is drowning.

☞ ALWAYS store pool chemicals away from petroleum products. Store all garden and outdoor chemicals and tools away from children.

☞ Label and store poisons safely. DO NOT store poisons in non-poison containers; NEVER store them in containers used for food or drink.

☞ DO NOT use poison containers for any other purpose.

☞ ALWAYS wear rubber gloves or another form of hand protection when handling any pesticides.

☞ DO NOT burn pesticide containers or aerosol cans in open fires or incinerators. DO NOT bury or deposit them in residential areas.

☞ DO NOT leave barbecues unattended.

☞ Play equipment and toys should suit the age of the child. Play equipment should have a soft surface beneath it and be checked regularly for hazards.

FIRE PREVENTION

☞ Keep a special fire blanket or woollen blanket in the kitchen to smother small isolated fires such as burning oil.

☞ Be very careful when cooking food in oil or fat. It does not take much to ignite these substances. If the oil or fat begins to smoke, turn it off immediately.

☞ Fat and oil used on the stove for cooking can very easily catch alight. When cooking with these substances, be prepared for such an occurrence and have a lid, plate or fire blanket close at hand to smother the flames. If possible, turn the hot-plate off.

☞ NEVER move the container or pour water on the flames, this will only worsen the situation by fanning the fire.

☞ Keep a fire extinguisher in a cool, easily accessible place.

☞ Turn all electrical appliances off at the wall during electrical storms.

☞ In the case of an electrical fire, switch electricity off at the power point and put the fire out with an extinguisher designed for electrical fires. If an extinguisher is unavailable, smother the fire with a woollen blanket or heavy rug.

☞ NEVER use water unless you are SURE the electrical current has been turned off.

Evacuation Procedures

☞ Work out an evacuation plan from all rooms in the house and make sure all household members are familiar with the plan.

☞ Create a meeting place outside where all household members can assemble.

☞ If the fire is impossible to extinguish turn off electricity and, if possible, shut all windows and doors to prevent draughts fanning the flames.

☞ Ring the fire brigade and emergency services from a close neighbour's telephone.

POINTS TO REMEMBER IN FIRST AID SITUATIONS

If you have to administer first aid, there are a number of points worthwhile remembering.

☞ If you are at all uncertain about a person's condition or the seriousness of the injury, seek immediate medical aid.

☞ If possible, always have the most experienced person look after the casualty while another goes for help.

☞ DO NOT leave a casualty unless you are the only person there, and there is little chance anyone will arrive for some time. Before going for help, treat a person's injuries or condition as best you can and make him/her as comfortable as possible.

☞ If there is more than one casualty, treat the most seriously injured first.

☞ If a person has more than one injury, treat the most serious injury first.

☞ Your message to the appropriate emergency medical services should be short and to the point. After delivering your message you should make sure it has been fully understood.

☞ When making an emergency telephone call, give:
– A contact telephone number.
– The exact location of the accident with directions on how to get there.
– The nature of the incident and the time it happened.
– A quick rundown on the number of casualties and their conditions.

☞ For your own benefit, ask how long medical aid will take to arrive.

☞ In the event of an accident, the best advice is to be prepared. It is only by doing a recognised first aid course that you can acquire the appropriate practical skills and become confident in treating an injured person. For more information on first aid courses or first aid books, contact your local St John Ambulance Centre.

RESCUING AN ELECTRIC SHOCK VICTIM

If a person has been electrocuted by a kitchen or household appliance:

☞ DO NOT touch the person until the current has been turned off or removed. This can be done by turning the power off at the power point, pulling the appliance cord free or removing the person from the current using non-conducting, dry materials such as a dry wooden broom stick.

☞ NEVER cut the electrical cord.

A FAMILY FIRST AID KIT

It is a good idea to have a first aid kit for your home. Although many household items can be used as substitutes in emergency situations, it is always better to be prepared and have a proper first aid kit on hand.

Check your first aid kit regularly to make sure it remains well stocked, and replace kit items, such as bandaids, safety pins and bandages, as they are used. Label the kit clearly and store it well away from wet areas – moisture will stain and ruin first aid materials. Keep the kit in an obvious place and make sure all family members know where it is.

A basic first aid kit should contain things such as:

ANTISEPTIC: a mild antiseptic cream used to sterilise and sooth a wound.

BANDAGES: this should include crepe bandages for sprains and strains; bandaids for minor cuts and scratches and material bandages used to control bleeding, keep dressings from moving, support an injury and confine movement or immobilize broken bones, sprains etc.

DRESSINGS: these should always be sterile (germ-free) and non-stick when using on a wound. They are used to sterilise wounds, keep them clean and protect them from infection. When buying dressings, always make sure the seal on the package is unbroken.

PADS: to be used over a dressing to apply pressure to the injury without risking infection through direct contact.

SAFETY PINS: to secure bandaging, slings, and so on.

SCISSORS: should only be small and easy to use in order to fit comfortably into the kit. Used to cut bandages, pads and so on.

TWEEZERS: to extract splinters and dirt from a minor wound.

NOTE: a complete family first aid kit is available from St John Ambulance Australia for about $65.00.

Household Substitutes

It is possible to improvise to some extent, with many common household items. These could include:

☞ Nappy pins.

☞ Piece of clean cloth or handkerchief to clean wounds (St John Ambulance Australia recommends against using cotton wool or tissue on wounds because these can stick to blood).

☞ Pillows on which to rest an injury.

☞ Clothing, such as ties, scarves, pantyhose and belts. A belt can be used as a makeshift sling or to support a sprained ankle. Scarves folded in half diagonally also make good arm slings.

☞ Towels.

☞ Sticky tape as a substitute for safety pins.

☞ An instant icepack can be made from a packet of peas, iceblocks wrapped in plastic bags and tea-towel, or anything else in your freezer that can change shape to rest comfortably on an injured part. However, make sure these are ALWAYS wrapped in a cloth or towel before being used on the skin, otherwise, frostbite may occur. See page 115 for instructions on how to make a useful icepack at home.

☞ Broom handles, umbrellas, rolled up newspaper or anything else long and thin can be used as a temporary splint.

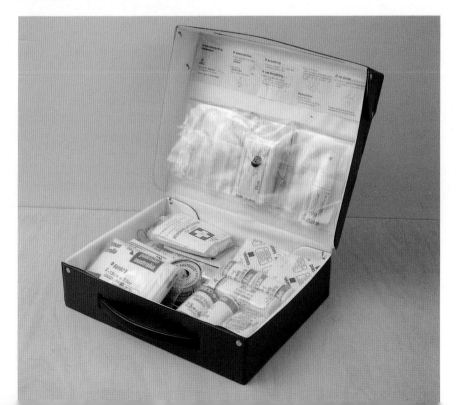

🖝 Check the person's airway is clear and open, check the person is breathing and has a heartbeat (to do this, see below). If breathing or circulation is absent, see Expired Air Resuscitation, at right, and Cardiopulmonary Resuscitation Techniques, page 113.

🖝 If the sufferer is conscious, help them into the most comfortable position, usually an upright sitting position.

🖝 Reassure the person.

🖝 Help the person with any medications that have been prescribed for their asthma attacks.

🖝 Ensure adequate fresh air.

🖝 Seek medical aid immediately.

Checking An Unconscious Person's Airway, Breathing And Circulation

1. If a person is unconscious, check their airpassage for any obstructions that may impede breathing. Sometimes an unconscious person's tongue may fall across their windpipe or the muscles along their windpipe may relax to block breathing. Clear the airway of any debris and open the airway by tilting the person's head back: placing one hand on their forehead and the other under their neck to extend the airway.

2. Check the person is breathing by placing your ear close to their mouth, listening and feeling for breath and watching their chest for movement.

If the person is breathing, place them in the stable side position (see page 116). If the person is NOT breathing, begin E.A.R. (see instructions at right).

3. To check for an adult's pulse, place your index and middle finger in the groove behind the Adam's apple.

To check for a child's pulse, place your hand over their heart.

If a heartbeat cannot be found, begin C.P.R. immediately (see page 113).

EXPIRED AIR RESUSCITATION (E.A.R.)

Mouth-to-Mouth Resuscitation (Adult)

1. Kneel beside the person.

2. Tilt the person's head back.

3. Pinch the person's nostrils to stop air from escaping through the nose.

4. With your other hand, open the person's mouth by pulling the jaw upwards using thumb below the bottom lip and forefinger under the chin in a pistol-like grip.

5. Take a deep breath and seal your mouth over the person's mouth.

6. Breathe into their mouth.

7. Remove your mouth and turn your head to watch the chest fall. Listen for the release of air as the person's lungs exhale air.

8. If the chest does not rise and fall, check the person's head tilt position to make sure the airpassage is open. Then check for any foreign objects which may be obstructing the airpassage.

9. Give 5 full breaths in 10 seconds, then check the person's neck pulse.

If a pulse is present, continue resuscitation at the rate of 1 breath every 4 seconds.

Mouth-to-Mouth Resuscitation – (Babies and Children under 8 yrs)

1. Make sure the airpassage is clear.

2. DO NOT tilt the head back but support the jaw.

3. DO NOT put pressure on the soft tissues under the child's chin.

4. Cover the child's mouth and nose with your mouth and puff gently using enough pressure to make the child's chest rise. Too much pressure may swell the stomach.

5. Continue with 1 breath every 3 seconds until medical aid arrives or the child starts to breathe.

5

7

CARDOPULMONARY RESUSCITATION (C.P.R.)

No matter how inexperienced you are at C.P.R., if a person is not breathing and has no heartbeat, you should try to give C.P.R. That is, unless there is a more experienced person on the scene. Be aware that even if C.P.R. is carried out properly it may not always be successful in saving a life. Success depends on the cause and extent of the injury, how quickly you respond to the situation and how soon medical help arrives.

Cardiopulmonary Resuscitation – (Adult)

1. If there is no pulse, kneel beside the person with one knee level with their chest and the other level with their head.

2. It is very important you carry out C.P.R. with your hands in the right position. This position can be found by:

☞ Finding the bottom of the breastbone at the base of the ribcage where both sides start to join.

☞ Locating the top of the breastbone by placing a finger in the hollow between the collarbones.

☞ Extending both thumbs equal distances from these points to meet in the middle.

☞ Keeping the thumb closest to the neck in place and positioning the heel of the other hand just below it.

3. Your fingers should be relaxed, slightly raised and pointing across the chest.

4. Secure your other hand firmly on top of the first by locking the top thumb around the bottom wrist or interlocking the fingers.

5. Apply pressure through the heel of your lower hand. Your shoulders should be above the person's breastbone and the arm applying the compression should be straight. Pivoting from the hips, perform the compressions rhythmically with equal time for compression and relaxation.

6. The breastbone should be pressed down about 5 centimetres before releasing pressure.

7. Give 15 quick compressions in 10-12 seconds. Then give two breaths in 3-5 seconds. Continue this with 4 cycles every minute until help arrives or the person regains a pulse.

2

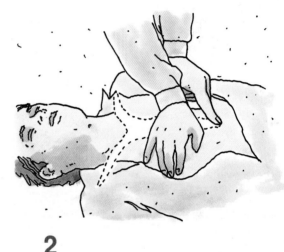

2

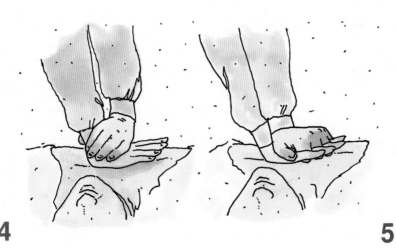

4

5

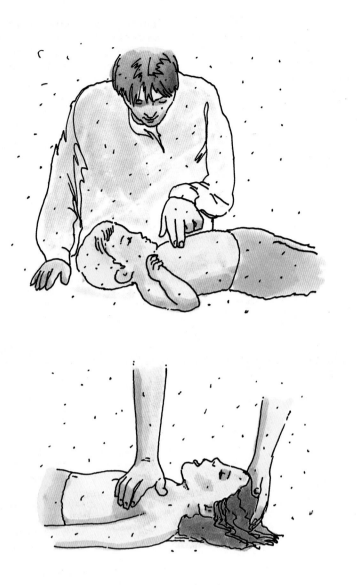

Cardiopulmonary Resuscitation – (Babies and Children under 8 yrs)

Under 12 months

Use two fingers on the middle of the breastbone.

Over 12 months

For a small child over 12 months old, use the heel of one hand for compression.

1. Give 2 quick breaths to every 15 compressions in 10 seconds. Continue this with 6 cycles every minute.

NOTE: If a person's breathing or heartbeat does not return while you are trying to resuscitate them, DONT STOP. It is important to continue resuscitation until medical aid arrives. By continuing to supply their system with oxygen, you at least give them a chance until they get to a hospital, or medical aid arrives.

BITES AND STINGS

Usually, non-lethal bites and stings of insects such as the bee, centipede, European wasp, red back spider and scorpion are treated by wiping the area clean and applying an ice pack. In the case of a bee sting, remove sting by scraping it sideways with a fingernail.

If there are signs of allergy, or if the person has an allergic history, treat using appropriate medication or seek immediate medical aid.

Emergency first aid advice for marine stings is available from the Marine Stinger Reporting Service on 008 079 909.

Bee Sting
See instructions above.

Blue Bottle

- Check the person's airway is clear and open, check the person is breathing and has a heartbeat (to do this, see page 112). If breathing or circulation is absent, refer to Expired Air Resuscitation and Cardiopulmonary Resuscitation Techniques, pages 112,113.
- If tentacles remain, gently pick off with tweezers or fingers or wash off with water.
- Apply an icepack or crushed ice wrapped in a thin towel or cloth to sting to relieve pain.
- DO NOT rub the area.
- Seek medical aid.

Blue-Ringed Octopus

A blue-ringed octopus bite is normally painless so a person may not be aware they have been bitten.

SYMPTOMS
- Numbness of the tongue and lips within minutes of being bitten.
- Pale and clammy skin.
- Extreme thirst.
- No breathing.

TREATMENT
- Check the person's airway is clear and open, check the person is breathing and has a heartbeat (to do this, see page 112). If breathing or circulation is absent, refer to Expired Air Resuscitation and Cardiopulmonary Resuscitation Techniques, pages 112, 113.
- Reassure the casualty.
- Begin E.A.R. as breathing becomes difficult (see page 112).
- Apply a pressure immobilisation bandage over the bitten area (see page 115).

Funnel-Web Spider

SYMPTOMS
- Intense pain at the site of the bite at first.
- Nausea, vomiting and stomach pain.
- Difficult and noisy breathing.
- Muscular weakness.
- Sweating and saliva from the mouth.
- Cold skin and numbness.
- Weeping from the eyes, cold skin and shivering.
- Coughing up secretions.

TREATMENT
- Check the person's airway is clear and open, check the person is breathing and has a heartbeat (to do this, see page 112). If breathing or circulation is absent, refer to Expired Air Resuscitation and Cardiopulmonary Resuscitation Techniques, pages 112, 113.
- Rest and reassure the person.
- Apply a pressure immobilization bandage (see page 115) over the bitten area and around the limb.
- Seek medical aid immediately.

Jellyfish
See Blue Bottle.

Snakes

Symptoms of snake bites appear between 15 minutes and 2 hours after the person has been bitten.

SYMPTOMS

- ✏ Puncture marks about 1 centimetre apart at the site of the bite.
- ✏ Swelling and reddening of the bitten area.
- ✏ Headache.
- ✏ Double vision.
- ✏ Drowsiness.
- ✏ Nausea, vomiting and diarrhoea.
- ✏ Pain or tightness in the chest or abdomen.
- ✏ Dizziness or faintness.
- ✏ Bruising around bitten area.
- ✏ Sweating.
- ✏ Breathing difficulties.

TREATMENT

- ✏ Check the person's airway is clear and open, check the person is breathing and has a heartbeat (to do this, see page 112). If breathing or circulation is absent, refer to Expired Air Resuscitation and Cardiopulmonary Resuscitation Techniques, pages 112, 113.
- ✏ Rest and reassure the person.
- ✏ Apply a pressure immobilisation bandage (see instructions at right) over the bitten area and around the limb.
- ✏ Seek medical aid immediately.

Tick

If in the ear or in an awkward-to-get-at place, seek medical aid.

If you can reach the tick remove it by sliding the open blades of a pair of small sharp scissors or tweezers down each side of the tick, and levering the tick outwards. Be careful not to leave the mouth parts of the tick in the skin.

Search carefully for other ticks on the body, particularly in the hair, behind the ears and in other body crevices.

If the person does not recover after a few hours or if a child is affected by a tick seek medical aid.

PRESSURE IMMOBILISATION

When applying pressure immobilisation it is best to use a crepe or conforming bandage. If this is unavailable, use pantyhose or other stretch material.

1. Apply the bandage firmly enough to compress tissue, but not so firm as to restrict the flow of blood to the limb below the bandage.

2. Bandage from the bite to the base of the limb (to the fingers or toes), then up to the top of the limb (to the armpit or groin). When bandaging an arm, first bend the elbow at 90 degrees.

3. Bandage as much of the injured limb as possible.

4. Apply a splint to the bandaged limb with a second bandage. The splint can be made of any firm material.

5. DO NOT remove the splint or bandage once applied.

BLEEDING WOUNDS

Cuts , scratches, grazes and splinters may be the most common of all household injuries. Who hasn't cut their finger while preparing food, fallen and scratched their knee, or got a splinter embedded while gardening. To avoid these minor cuts and scratches becoming serious and/or infected, a number of simple points should be put into practice:

- ✏ Wash hands thoroughly before and after treating an injury.
- ✏ Clean the wound as well as possible using a clean antiseptic cloth, moistened handkerchief or by washing under cold running water. The cold water will also slow down the blood flow.
- ✏ Once bleeding is under control you may clean around the wound with a mild soap and water and a swab of cotton wool. Use a clean part of the cotton wool swab each stroke, to avoid infection. DO NOT wash or wipe away blood clots. These form to prevent further bleeding.
- ✏ For minor injuries, any dirt or foreign matter on the surface of the wound and around it can be removed by dabbing with a sterile cloth, running under water, or using sterile tweezers. DO NOT use tweezers or any other utensil to dig into the wound as this may worsen it.
- ✏ If you have any doubts about the seriousness of the wound or it reddens, swells and/or becomes pussy over the next

few days, it could be infected so consult your doctor as soon as possible.

- ✏ If the wound is dirty, make certain the person is up to date with their tetanus injection. If not, they may need to get a shot immediately.
- ✏ Always cover wounds with a clean or sterile, non-stick dressing. If a dressing is not available, put on a piece of gauze followed by a swab of cotton wool before applying the bandage. DO NOT apply dry cotton wool directly onto a wound – it may stick.

FOR MORE SEVERE EXTERNAL BLEEDING:

- ✏ Lie the person down and apply direct pressure to the bleeding area with fingers or hand.
- ✏ Loosen all tight clothing and raise the injured area if possible.
- ✏ Apply a clean dressing over the wound as soon as possible, followed by a pad big enough to cover the wound.
- ✏ Seek medical aid immediately.

BROKEN BONES

See Fractures.

BRUISES

Raise the injured part and hold under cold running water for at least 10 minutes to slow down the flow of blood through the area. Better still, place an icepack over the bruise.

St John Ambulance recommends holding an icepack on the bruised area for 20 minutes and reapplying every 2 hours, for the first 24 hours, and every 4 hours for a further 24 hours.

If the bruising is bad, compression bandages should be applied covering an area well beyond the bruised area. Bad bruising could indicate serious internal bleeding and a sharp or heavy blow can cause injury to an underlying bone. If you are at all concerned about the injury, seek medical aid.

HOMEMADE ICEPACK

An icepack can be made easily with ice cubes out of the freezer, a plastic bag, some salt and a tea-towel. Sprinkle ice cubes liberally with salt to increase its melting point. Tie the bag firmly shut to avoid it leaking and wrap in a tea-towel, towel or cloth. ALWAYS wrap an icepack in a cloth or towel before using it on a person's skin, otherwise frostbite may occur.

BURNS

Burns can be very dangerous, even fatal, depending on their extent. St John Ambulance recommends medical aid if the burn is larger than a 20 cent piece and blisters. However, if the casualty is a young baby or a sick older person, always seek medical aid. Seek immediate medical aid if:

☞ The burn is deep – the skin looks white or black and charred (the casualty may not feel any pain).

☞ The burn involves the airway, hands, face or genitals.

☞ You are unsure how serious the burn is.

TREATMENT

☞ Cool the burnt area by running it under cold running water or immersing in a bowl of cool water for up to 10 minutes. Cooling a wound can minimise the damage and offer relief to the casualty.

☞ Carefully remove any jewellery or clothing from around the wound before it starts to swell. DO NOT remove any materials stuck to the burnt area.

☞ Cover the burn with a sterile dressing larger than the wound or a clean non-fluffy material to minimise infection.

☞ In the case of serious burns, treat the patient for shock (see page 120) as they may also suffer severe fluid loss.

☞ If the person is conscious and thirsty allow small amounts of water.

☞ Soothe extreme pain by pouring cold water over the dressing.

☞ DO NOT attempt to cool or relieve the burn with butter, fats, lotions, ointments or any other oily dressing. These substances will absorb heat and make the burn worse.

☞ DO NOT interfere with the burn by breaking blisters, removing loose skin or removing anything stuck to the burn. Burns can get infected very easily

☞ DO NOT give alcohol to drink.

☞ DO NOT overcool the casualty, especially if very young or if the burnt area is extensive. Overcooling can be indicated by the person shivering.

☞ DO NOT use towels, cotton wool, blankets or adhesive dressings directly on the burn.

RESCUING A BURNT PERSON

If entering a burning building

☞ Feel the temperature of the door. If it's hot DO NOT enter. If cold or slightly warm, crouch low and open the door slowly.

☞ Cover mouth and nose with a damp cloth to avoid smoke inhalation.

☞ If a person's clothing is on fire, make them lie on the ground so that the flames are kept away from their head, and smother the flames with a wool blanket, heavy jacket or water.

☞ DO NOT try to douse the flames by rolling the person on the ground. This serves only to burn the person further and spread the flames.

☞ DO NOT use flammable materials to smother the flames, the fibres will melt and give the person severe burns.

SUNBURN

Sunburn can be as serious as any other type of burn.

☞ Avoid sunbaking between 10am and 3pm when the sun's rays are most harmful.

☞ Wear a wide brimmed hat, a suitable sunscreen and a T-shirt when out in the sun.

☞ Apply cool, moist compresses to the sunburned areas.

☞ Make sure the person rests in a cool, shady place.

☞ Give the person lots of liquids to drink.

☞ Seek medical attention if the sunburn is severe or if a baby is sunburnt – the loss of fluid in a baby can quickly lead to shock.

☞ The sap from an aloe vera leaf rubbed gently onto minor sunburn can offer relief to the sufferer.

Young children are more prone to choking because they enjoy putting all manner of things in their mouths. If you have young children in your house it is wise to check that small items such as jewellery, game pieces and coins are not left lying on the floor or anywhere in the reach of tiny hands. If you think a person is choking, act quickly.

SYMPTOMS

☞ Coughing.

☞ Violent attempts to breathe.

☞ Clutching the throat.

☞ Blueness of the face, neck, lips, ears and fingernails.

☞ Sometimes unconsciousness and loss of breathing.

TREATMENT

If the person is conscious and breathing:

☞ Encourage them to take deep, even breaths.

☞ Encourage them to cough, this may be enough to dislodge the obstruction.

☞ If this does not work, help the person to bend down low so their head is lower than their lungs. Give 3 or 4 sharp blows between the shoulder blades with the palm of your hand.

☞ If breathing is laboured, seek medical aid immediately.

☞ For a small child or baby, lay the child, stomach down, across your lap – supporting them with your arm – slap firmly between the shoulder blades.

☞ Check the mouth once again for the obstruction. If you can't see anything in their mouth, continue to slap the child's back and seek medical aid immediately.

If the person is breathing and unconscious:

☞ Place them in the stable side position (see instructions below).

☞ Seek medical aid immediately.

If the person is not breathing:

☞ Check the person's airway is clear and open, check the person has a heartbeat (to do this, see page 112). If breathing or circulation is absent, refer to Expired Air Resuscitation and Cardiopulmonary Resuscitation Techniques, pages 112, 113.

☞ Check the mouth for any obstruction. If it is visible, try to dislodge it with you forefinger and index finger. If the obstruction is not visible DO NOT probe deeply with your finger, you could injure the person's throat. DO NOT push the obstruction further down the throat.

☞ Seek medical aid immediately.

STABLE SIDE POSITION

If a person is breathing but unconscious, gently place them into the stable side position. This ensures the person's airpassage remains open and allows any vomit or other body fluid to drain away freely, without risk of choking. If an unconscious person is already on their side or lying on their stomach, leave them in that position.

1. Gently turn the person's neck towards you. Keep the airpassage open by extending the jaw forward.

2. Place the arm nearest you flat on the ground, palm up and nestled into the person's side.

3. Bend the person's furthest arm at the elbow and position across their chest.

4. Cross the person's furthest ankle over the other.

5. Gently roll the person towards you onto their side, supporting their head and neck and pulling from the hips. If the person is heavy, this is best done by holding onto a piece of clothing.

6. Check the head is still in a position to allow a free and open airpassage.

7. Extend the bent arm out to rest at right angles to the body, palm down. This will serve to prevent the upper body from rolling forward.

8. Bend the top leg at the knee and position at right angles to the body. This will serve

to prevent the lower half of the body from rolling forward.

9. Position the remaining arm behind the casualty, palm up. This will serve to prevent the casualty rolling onto their back.

CONVULSIONS

This condition can happen to young children and babies and may be caused by a high body temperature brought on by sickness.

SYMPTOMS
- Stiff and rigid body.
- Twitching arms and legs.
- Rolling eyes.
- Lips and face turning blue.
- Coughing, choking and congestion.
- Unconsciousness.

TREATMENT
- Check the child's airway is clear and open, check the child is breathing and has a heartbeat (to do this, see page 112). If breathing or circulation is absent, refer to Expired Air Resuscitation and Cardiopulmonary Resuscitation Techniques, pages 112, 113.
- Remove all clothing.
- If the child feels hot, sponge their body down with water that is slightly cooler than body temperature (37 degrees Celcius).
- Fan the wet child with a newspaper to speed up the cooling process but make sure not to overcool. Overcooling can be indicated by shivering.
- When the child has stopped convulsing and his/her body temperature is back to normal, cover child lightly.
- Seek medical aid.

DIABETES

High Blood Sugar Levels

SYMPTOMS
- Excessive thirst.
- Frequent need to go to the toilet.
- Hot, dry skin.
- Rapid pulse.
- The smell of acetone on the breath (like nail polish remover).
- Drowsiness.
- Unconsciousness.

TREATMENT

If the person is unconscious
- Check the person's airway is clear and open, check the person is breathing and has a heartbeat (to do this, see page 112). If breathing or circulation is absent, refer to Expired Air Resuscitation and Cardiopulmonary Resuscitation Techniques, pages 112, 113.
- Place them in the stable side position (see page 116).
- Seek medical aid immediately.

If the person is conscious
- Allow the person to administer insulin themselves. DO NOT administer it yourself.
- Seek medical aid. If this is delayed, the person should drink sugar-free liquids.

Low Blood Sugar Levels

SYMPTOMS
- Dizziness.
- Weakness and shaking.
- Numb feeling in lips and fingers.
- Sweating and pallid complexion.
- Rapid pulse.
- Confusion.

TREATMENT

If the person is unconsious
- Check the person's airway is clear and

open, check the person is breathing and has a heartbeat (to do this, see page 112). If breathing or circulation is absent, refer to Expired Air Resuscitation and Cardiopulmonary Resuscitation Techniques, pages 112, 113.
- DO NOT give anything by mouth.
- Place person in the stable side position (see page 116).
- Seek medical aid immediately.

If the person is conscious
- Give sugar, glucose or a drink sweetened with lots of sugar, for example, a soft drink.
- Continue giving sugar every 15 minutes until medical aid arrives or the person recovers.
- Loosen tight clothing.
- Seek medical aid.

DROWNING

NOTE: if you are not a very strong swimmer, DO NOT attempt to rescue a drowning person from in the water, nobody wants two casualties or drowning victims.

TREATMENT
- Once out of the water, check the airway and begin E.A.R. (see page 112).
- If pulse is absent, begin C.P.R. (see page 113).
- If the person starts to breath, but is still unconscious, place them on their side in the stable side position (see page 116), keep the person warm and regularly observe and record their heart rate and breathing until medical help arrives.
- Seek medical aid immediately.

EAR INJURIES

Bleeding from the Ear
This could indicate a serious injury like a broken skull so seek medical aid immediately. Allow fluid to drain freely by placing the person on their side with the bleeding ear downwards. Place a clean pad between the ear and the ground.
- DO NOT plug the ear.
- DO NOT give ear drops.

Foreign Objects in the Ear
Gently inspect the ear to identify the object and how deep it is. Seek medical aid and DO NOT attempt to move the object unless it is an insect. If it is an insect, place a droplet of warm vegetable oil or water in the ear. If the insect does not float out, seek medical aid.

Ruptured Eardrum
SYMPTOMS
- Decrease in hearing.
- Usually severe pain.

- Blood or fluid escaping from the ear.

- Reassure the person.
- Treat as you would a bleeding ear.
- Seek immediate medical aid.

EPILEPTIC SEIZURES

- A "cry" as air is forced out through the vocal chords.
- The person collapses and lies rigid for some seconds with their back arched and jaws clenched.
- Blueness of the face and neck.
- Spasmodic muscular movement and colour improvement as breathing starts.
- Froth from the mouth, may be bloodstained.
- The person may bite their tongue.
- Loss of bladder and bowel control.
- The person regains consciousness but may be confused for several minutes and may be unaware of what happened.
- After the seizure the casualty may be exhausted and sleep deeply.

- DO NOT restrict movement but protect the person from injury by clearing the area around them of all injurious items such as sharp-edged furniture and objects.
- DO NOT attempt to put anything in the person's mouth.
- Place the person on their side as soon as possible.
- Treat any injuries that result from the seizure.
- If the person falls asleep, DO NOT disturb but continue to check airway, breathing and circulation.
- If you know the person is an epileptic seek medical aid only if the seizure continues for more than 10 minutes.

EYE INJURIES

If the person wears contact lenses which can be easily removed, ask them to take them out before treating an eye injury. DO NOT continue examining the eye if the injury is serious, seek immediate medical aid. Eyes can become infected easily so always wash your hands thoroughly before touching an injured person.

Burns to the Eye

- Pain.
- Watering eyes.
- Bloodshot eyeball.
- Swollen eyelids.
- Intolerance to light.

- Open eyelids with fingers gently.
- Wash the eye with cold, flowing water for at least 20 minutes, washing under both eyelids.
- Position eyepads or light, clean dressings over both eyes.
- Seek medical aid.

Foreign Object in the Eye

- DO NOT let the person rub their eye.
- DO NOT remove any object that is embedded in the eye.
- DO NOT try to remove any foreign matter from the coloured part of the eye.
- To remove, ask the person to look up and gently pull the lower lid down, and remove using the corner of a clean cloth moistened with water.
- If the foreign object is not visible you may be able to dislodge it by getting the person to look down and gently pulling the upper lid down and over the lower lid.
- If the methods described above are both unsuccessful, wash the eye under a gentle stream of water or sterile salt solution if handy.

Wounds to the Eyes

Lay the person on their back and cover both eyes with a light sterile dressing, ensuring the person does not move their eyes. Make certain there is no pressure on the injured eye.

FAINTING

Most fainting spells are usually brought on by the circumstances of the moment or the few hours leading up to it. Recovery is usually quick and complete but may be indicative of a more serious condition.

If someone complains of feeling faint or displays symptoms of dizziness, blurred vision or weakness, sit the person down, make them as comfortable as possible, loosen tight clothing, lower their head down between their knees and instruct the person to take deep, even breaths. Other symptoms of fainting may include:
- Dizziness.
- Blurred vision.
- Hot and cold feeling.
- Yawning.
- Temporary loss of consciousness.
- Slow, weak pulse.
- Pale, cold and clammy skin.

If a person collapses and looses consciousness

- Turn the person onto their back and raise their legs.
- Loosen all tight clothing.
- Check for injuries resulting from the fall and treat accordingly.
- After recovery, allow the person to rest for some minutes before moving.
- If the person does not recover quickly, seek medical aid. Check the person's airway is clear, check the person is breathing and has a heartbeat (to do this, see page 112). If breathing or circulation is absent, refer to Expired Air Resuscitation and Cardiopulmonary Resuscitation Techniques, pages 112, 113.

FRACTURES

It is often hard to distinguish between a broken bone, sprain, strain or dislocation – they all involve a great deal of pain. If you are at all unsure about the injury, treat it as a fracture In this way you will not worsen the injury by mistreating it.

- The break was felt or heard by the person.
- The person is suffering pain at or near the site of injury, which worsens when any attempts are made to move the injured part.
- The person finds it extremely difficult or impossible to move the injured part or areas around the injury.
- The injury looks deformed, abnormally twisted, shortened or is sticking out at an unnatural angle.
- The injured part and surrounding areas swell and look bruised.

- If the person is suffering from other, more serious wounds, treat them before treating the fracture. Likewise, control all bleeding and cover all wounds, if any.
- Make the person as comfortable as possible and handle the injured area very gently.
- Ensure the person does not move the injured part by immobilising the affected area with slings, bandages or splints. Make sure that whatever you use to immobilise the injured part does not cut off blood circulation to the area or cause extra pain.

If medical aid is soon to arrive, supporting the injured part with blankets and other soft padding will do. If an arm is injured and medical aid is on its way, ask the person to support the injured limb with their good arm.
- Move the person only if there is danger to you or the person.
- Observe the person closely and treat any signs of shock (see page 120).
- If possible, raise the injured part to slow down the flow of blood through the area and reduce swelling and discomfort.
- Watch closely that blood circulation to the injured part and areas around the injury does not cease.

HEART ATTACK

SYMPTOMS

- Pain or discomfort in the centre of the chest. This can be severe and stabbing and may radiate up the neck and jaw or down either arm.
- Anxiety, confusion or distress.
- Nausea and vomiting.
- Shortness of breath.
- Pallid and clammy skin.
- Sometimes an irregular pulse.
- Sometimes immediate collapse leading to no heart beat.
- Shock may develop as a secondary condition.

TREATMENT

- Check the person's airway is clear, check the person is breathing and has a heartbeat (to do this, see page 112). If breathing or circulation is absent, refer to Expired Air Resuscitation and Cardiopulmonary Resuscitation Techniques, pages 112, 113.
- Support the person in a sitting position.
- If the pulse is weak and rapid or the person is faint-headed, position the person on their side unless they are more comfortable sitting.
- If the person is unconscious, place them in the stable side position (see page 116).
- Seek medical aid immediately.

NOSE INJURIES

Bleeding from the Nose

- Instruct the person to breathe through their mouth and not to blow their nose.
- Sit the person up with their head tilted slightly forward.
- Have the person apply finger and thumb pressure on the soft part of the nostrils for at least 10 minutes.
- Loosen all tight clothing around the head, neck and waist.
- Keep the person cool with a good supply of fresh air.
- Place cold, wet towels on the neck and forehead.
- If bleeding continues, reapply finger and thumb pressure for a further 10 minutes. If bleeding continues, seek medical aid.

Broken Nose

If the broken nose is bleeding, treat as a bleeding nose. DO NOT apply pressure unless bleeding is severe.

Foreign Object in the Nose

Block the opposite nostril and get the person to blow out their nose.

Tell the person to breathe in through their mouth.

OVERBREATHING

SYMPTOMS

- Feeling of choking, suffocation and a need to breath deeply.
- Anxiety.
- Tingling feeling in hands, feet and face.

TREATMENT

- Reassure the person.
- Encourage the person to take slow, regular breaths.
- Instruct the person to breathe in and out of a paper bag until symptoms disappear.

OVER EXPOSURE TO HEAT

A healthy human body maintains a normal temperature of 37 degrees Celsius.

Young children, the elderly, people wearing unsuitable clothing at work or while exercising and people who work in hot climates, are more at risk in suffering from overexposure to heat.

SYMPTOMS

- Feeling hot, exhausted and weak, with a headache which may have persisted for some hours or days.
- Vomiting or nauseous feeling.
- Tiredness, dizziness or weakness.
- Extreme thirst.
- Loss of appetite.
- Pallid, cool and clammy skin.
- Profuse sweating.
- Rapid breathing and pulse with possible shortness of breath.
- Lack of co-ordination.
- Possible confusion or irritability.
- Stomach and muscle cramps.

TREATMENT

- Move the person to a cool place and make them lie down.
- Replace lost fluids by giving plenty of water with glucose or sugar in small amounts, and half a teaspoon of salt per litre of water may be added.
- Loosen any tight clothing and remove any unnecessary clothes.
- Sponge the body down with cold water but DO NOT overcool. Overcooling can be indicated by shivering.

In the case of heat stroke victims, apply cold packs or ice to the areas of large blood vessels such as the neck, groin and armpits to accelerate cooling.

- When the person is fully conscious give fluids to drink.

POISONING

If you suspect a person has been poisoned, contact a Poisons Information Centre (numbers listed in Emergency Numbers chart, page 122) for advice on the treatment of a specific poison. If you are unsure about the type of poison, seek medical aid immediately, save specimens of vomit, pills, substances or empty containers found near the person, to give to medical personnel. Anything that could help a doctor determine what poison was taken, how much and when, should accompany the person to hospital.

Help is available on State Poisons Information Centre numbers 24 hours a day, or you can phone the national toll free Poisons Information Centre line.

National Poisons Information Line: (008) 25 1525 answers 24 hours

SYMPTOMS

These vary with the nature and type of poison causing the condition. The following may occur:

- Abdominal pain.
- Vomiting.
- Drowsiness.
- Burning pains from the mouth to the stomach.
- Breathing difficulties.
- Constricting chest pains.
- Headache.
- Ringing in the ears.
- Blurred vision.
- A smell of fumes.
- Odours on the breath.
- Bite or injection marks with or without swelling around the area.
- Contamination of the skin.
- Blueness of the lips and change of normal skin colour.
- Burns around the mouth and inside.

TREATMENT

- DO NOT induce vomiting, seek medical aid immediately.
- Call the Fire Brigade if the atmosphere is contaminated with smoke, gases or ammonia.
- If the person stops breathing, carry out E.A.R. (see page 112).
- If the person begins breathing but remains unconscious, place in the stable side position (see page 116).
- Seek medical aid immediately.

SHOCK

Shock can result from serious injury or illness, especially when there has been pain, heavy bleeding, or a serious loss of body fluids – as in the case of burns.

Shock may not become obvious immediately after an injury. Symptoms can develop over a period of time and will depend on the seriousness of the injury. A person suffering from shock will initially display such symptoms as:

- Pale face, lips and fingernails.
- Rapid breathing and pulse.
- Cold, clammy skin.
- A faint or dizzy feeling.
- Nausea or vomiting.
- Restlessness and excessive thirst.
- Extremities turning a blueish colour.
- Drowsiness, confusion or perhaps unconsciousness.

TREATMENT
- Lay the person down and raise their legs above the level of their heart
- Check the person's airway is clear, check the person is breathing and has a heartbeat (to do this, see page 112) and treat any wounds or injuries. If breathing or circulation is absent, refer to Expired Air Resuscitation and Cardiopulmonary Resuscitation Techniques, pages 112,113.
- Loosen all tight clothing.
- Make the person as comfortable as possible and maintain their normal body warmth.
- If the person is thirsty, moisten their lips, otherwise, don't give anything to eat or drink.

SPLINTERS

- Use only sterilised tweezers to remove the splinter. Tweezers can be quickly sterilised by immersing in concentrated disenfectant or holding the tip under a flame. DO NOT touch the end of the tweezers after sterilising.
- Try grasping the end of the splinter and removing it the same way it went in. If the splinter is deeply embedded, DO NOT "dig" around the opening to get at it rather, consult your doctor to have it removed.
- If the splinter is dirty, the person may need to have a tetanus injection.

SPRAINS

A sprain occurs when ligaments and tissues around a joint are stretched or torn.

SYMPTOMS
- Pain which may restrict movement and use of limb.
- Swelling and bruising.

TREATMENT
- If you are unsure about the injury, treat as a fracture – it is often difficult to tell the difference between a sprain and a broken bone.
- Apply an icepack to the injured area (see page 115 for instructions on how to make an icepack at home).
- Raise the sprained area and support in a comfortable way.
- Once swelling has gone down, support the area with a thick layer of cotton wool under a crepe bandage.
- If the person is suffering a sprained ankle, do not remove their shoe - it will serve to add extra support to the injured part.

STRAINS

A strain occurs when a muscle or tendon is overstretched or pulled a little too far.

SYMPTOMS
- Pain in the affected area, which starts suddenly.
- Pain when muscle is moved or stretched.
- Tenderness around the area and loss of strength.

TREATMENT
- Apply an icepack over the area to relieve the pain (see page 115 for instructions on how to make an icepack at home).
- As the muscle softens, replace the icepack with a warm hot-water bottle wrapped in a towel.
- Rest the injured part making certain the person does not further overstretch the muscle or tendon.
- Support the injured part with a crepe bandage.
- Encourage gentle exercise to reduce painful muscular spasms and shortening of the muscle.
- DO NOT rub or massage the affected area.

STROKE

SYMPTOMS
- Loss of movement and feeling, usually on one side of the body.
- Severe headache and weakness.
- Difficulty in swallowing.
- Slurred or unclear speech.
- Flushed face.
- Possibility of the head and eyes turned to one side.
- Pupils may be different sizes.
- Pounding pulse.

TREATMENT
- Check the person's airway is clear, check the person is breathing and has a heartbeat (to do this, see page 112). If breathing or circulation is absent, refer to Expired Air Resuscitation and Cardiopulmonary Resuscitation Techniques, pages 112, 113.
- Seek medical aid immediately.
- Reassure the person. They may be able to understand you even if unable to communicate.
- If the person is conscious, support the head and shoulders on pillows, loosen tight clothing, maintain normal body temperature and wipe away any fluids from the mouth.
- Make sure the airway is clear and open at all times.
- If the person is breathing but unconscious, place in the stable side position (see page 116).

TOOTH INJURIES

Bleeding from a Tooth Socket
- Instruct the person to keep their tongue clear of the socket.
- DO NOT remove the clot from the socket by rinsing the mouth.
- Place a firm pad of gauze over the socket and instruct the person to bite down firmly on the pad.
- If the bleeding continues seek medical or dental aid.

Loosing a Tooth
If a tooth is knocked out, save the tooth and clean it by washing it in saliva or milk or having the person suck on it. DO NOT handle the tooth or wash it any other way as this may kill the bacteria in the tooth and ruin any chances of being able to replace it. If possible, place the tooth back in its original position as soon as possible and seek medical or dental aid immediately.

First aid material in this chapter was compiled with the assistance of St John Ambulance Australia. More detailed first aid information is contained in the *Australian First Aid Manual, Volume One*, published by St John Ambulance Australia and available from any St John Ambulance centre. They also teach first aid courses and sell a range of first aid kits suitable for the home and workplace.

Safety tips compiled with the assistance of the Child Safety Unit, Camperdown Children's Hospital, Sydney.

Name

Date of Birth

Blood Group

Important illnesses and operations

Illness	Date	Treatment	Doctor

Allergies

Type	Aggravated by	Treatment

Immunisations

Immunisation is a simple, effective method of protecting your children from catching dangerous diseases. The course does not need to be repeated from the beginning if it has been interrupted. Two months is the recommended starting age but immunisation is as effective in older children. Parents are advised to start immunisation early because whooping cough is most serious in young babies.

Immunisation Date:

Triple Antigen: protection against diptheria, whooping cough and tetanus (at 2 months, 4 months, 6 months of age)	yes/no
Sabin oral vaccine: protection against poliomyelitis (at 2 months, 4 months, 6 months of age)	yes/no
Measles vaccine: may be given separately or with mumps vaccine (at 12 to 15 months of age)	yes/no
Mumps vaccine : may be given separately or combined with measles vaccine (at 12 to 15 months of age)	yes/no
Diptheria and tetanus booster, plus Sabin oral vaccine (at 18 months of age, pre-school or school entry)	yes/no
Rubella /German measles (girls 12 to 14 years)	yes/no
Booster injection of adult diptheria and tetanus vaccine (ADT) (at 15 years of age or on leaving school)	yes/no
Booster dose of Sabin oral vaccine	yes/no
Other immunisations	

EMERGENCY NUMBERS

Keep a list of important telephone numbers which can be referred to quickly and easily in cases of an emergency.
The list should include the following numbers:

AMBULANCE ☎ . . . .

FIRE BRIGADE ☎ . . . .

POLICE ☎ . . . .

Poisons Information Centres

National 24 hour Poisons Information Hotline toll free   (008) 25 1525

CANBERRA (A.C.T.)	☎ (06) 243 2154
NEW SOUTH WALES	☎ (02) 519 0466
NORTHERN TERRITORY	☎ (089) 228 888
QUEENSLAND	☎ (07) 253 8233
SOUTH AUSTRALIA	☎ (08) 267 7000
TASMANIA	☎ (002) 388 485
VICTORIA	☎ (03) 345 5678
WESTERN AUSTRALIA	☎ (09) 381 1177

Other important numbers

NEAREST NEIGHBOUR WITH A CAR ☎ . . . . .name: . . . .

NEAREST HOSPITAL ☎ . . . . .name: . . . .

   Emergency ☎ . . . . .name: . . . .

   General Enquiries ☎ . . . . .name: . . . .

   Nearest Children's Hospital ☎ . . . . .name: . . . .

FAMILY DOCTOR ☎ . . . . .name: . . . .

   Office Hours ☎ . . . . .name: . . . .

   After Hours ☎ . . . . .name: . . . .

NEAREST CHEMIST / PHARMACY ☎ . . . . .name . . . .

   After Hours Chemist/Pharmacy ☎ . . . . .name: . . . .

FAMILY DENTIST ☎ . . . . .name: . . . .

   Office Hours ☎ . . . . .name: . . . .

   After Hours ☎ . . . . .name: . . . .

BABY- SITTER ☎ . . . . .name: . . . .

LOCAL COUNCIL ☎ . . . . .name: . . . .

NUMBERS TO REMEMBER

AIR-CONDITIONING MECHANIC: ☎ . . . . .name . . . .

BUILDER: ☎ . . . . .name: . . . .

CARPET LAYER: ☎ . . . . .name: . . . .

DISHWASHER REPAIRS: ☎ . . . . .name: . . . .

ELECTRICIAN: ☎ . . . . .name: . . . .

ELECTRICITY AUTHORITY: ☎ . . . . .name: . . . .

GAS AUTHORITY: ☎ . . . . .name: . . . .

GARDENER: ☎ . . . . .name: . . . .

GLAZIER (glass repairs): ☎ . . . . .name: . . . .

HANDYMAN: ☎ . . . . .name: . . . .

HARDWARE STORE: ☎ . . . . .name: . . . .

HEATING REPAIRS: ☎ . . . . .name: . . . .

PLUMBER: ☎ . . . . .name: . . . .

PAINTER: ☎ . . . . .name: . . . .

   Bathroom: Paint type: . . . . colour: . . . .

   Bedrooms: Paint type: . . . . colour: . . . .

   Hallway: Paint type: . . . . colour: . . . .

   Kitchen: Paint type: . . . . colour: . . . .

   Lounge/ Sitting Room: Paint type: . . . . colour: . . . .

   Outdoor Areas: Paint type: . . . . colour: . . . .

REFRIGERATOR REPAIRS: ☎ . . . . .name: . . . .

TELEVISION / VCR REPAIRS: ☎ . . . . .name: . . . .

TILER: ☎ . . . . .name: . . . .

   Bathroom: Tile type: . . . . colour: . . . .

   Entry Hall: Tile type: . . . . colour: . . . .

   Kitchen: Tile type: . . . . colour: . . . .

   Bedrooms: Tile type: . . . . colour: . . . .

   Dining Room: Tile type: . . . . colour: . . . .

   Hallway: Tile type: . . . . colour: . . . .

   Kitchen: Tile type: . . . . colour: . . . .

   Lounge/ Sitting Room: Tile type: . . . . colour . . . .

WALLPAPERER: ☎ . . . . .name: . . . .

WASHING MACHINE REPAIRS: ☎ . . . . .name: . . . .

WATER BOARD: ☎ . . . . .name: . . . .

INDEX